The Family Tree of Fractal Curv

A taxonomy of plane-filling curves using con

Jeffrey Ventrella

Ventrella, Jeffrey

The Family Tree of Fractal Curves

First edition (July, 2019)

www.fractalcurves.com

ISBN 978-0-9830546-3-4

Eyebrain Books

www.eyebrainbooks.com

Tsunami curve

Contents

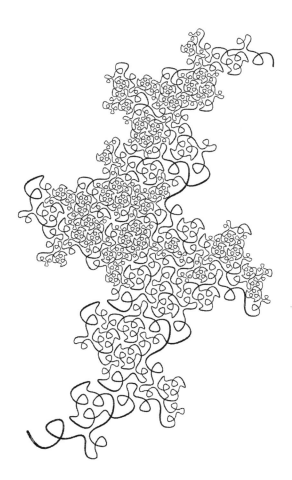

Acknowledgments

I would like to thank Vince Matsko for his in-depth review, advice, and editing from the perspective of a math educator. I would also like to thank Linda Jay for her copyediting work. Thanks to brother Philip, Scott Bowling, and Wayne Bollinger for early creative explorations. Much thanks to Dr. David Burton for ideas at the intersection of math and art. Thank you Kirk Israel for advice and suggestions. Thank you Julia Smith for creative sessions in exploring the taxonomies of fractal curves. Much gratitude goes out to the following people: Scott Kim, Gary Walker, Beth O'Sullivan, Gary Teachout, Henry Segerman, David Olsen, Christoph Bandt, Jörg Arndt, Benjamin Trube, Craig Kaplan, Eddie Elliot, David Mitchell, and Ed Zajec. I would like to thank Adam Goucher for pointing me to the rich universe of complex integer lattices, and for reviewing a draft of the book. And finally, thanks to Nuala Creed, for her continual support and love.

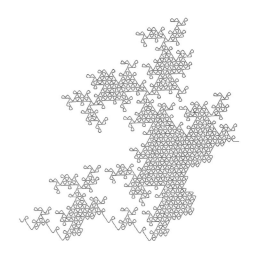

A personal note on the math in this book

This book is intended for college-educated readers who share a fascination with geometry, fractals, and number theory. My schooling did not include math other than the bare minimum requirements. My journey began in the practice of visual art. I happened upon fractals and computer programming as part of an exploration in visual expression through algorithms. When I first laid my eyes on Mandelbrot's book, *The Fractal Geometry of Nature*, I was struck by the illustrations of strange, novel forms. Over the years, I would periodically return to the book for a fresh look. Each time, I would engage in a bit more of the text, which expanded my vocabulary…and my collection of books. The math gradually began to take shape. The illustrations in Mandelbrot's book served as my initial impetus to learn more. As a visual thinker, this was my catalyst for attaining knowledge. This journey has resulted in many thousands of hand-drawn diagrams and a lot of software, developed over the span of more than three decades. It became a lifelong obsession.

I have always wanted to write a book that triggers the same curiosity and wonder that I had experienced…for readers who are not necessarily trained in math—because I knew from personal experience that any curious mind could be stimulated to experience math—through pictures and words. This book uses very little math notation, and there are no proofs. There are several conjectures. In some parts of the book I venture out a bit beyond my normal comfort zone—a risk I consider worth taking. I would encourage any reader to work out proofs and generalizations—to take over where I have left off.

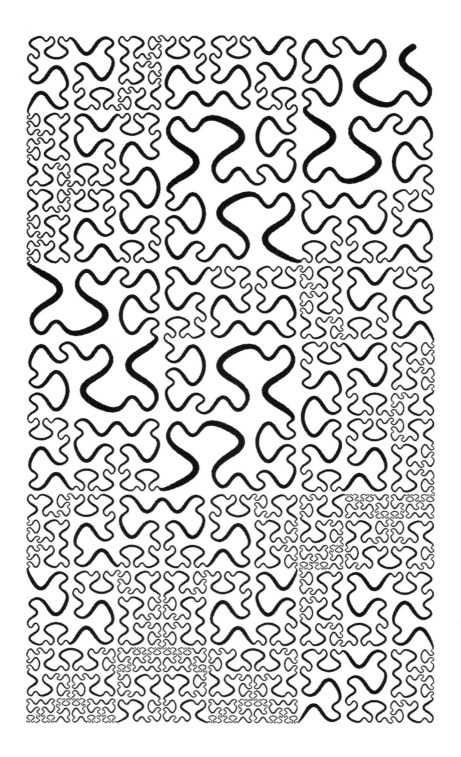

1

Introduction

Imagine that you are a paleontologist. You set sail to a remote island to find fossils. When you arrive at the shore, you quickly begin searching. Then you happen upon a rocky plain with strange-looking fossils. Preserved in the rocks are numerous organic shapes, indicating that several remarkable species once flourished on this island. Although the shapes have magnificent variation, there are also some common themes, body shapes, and patterns. The fossils are well-preserved, and you can even detect complicated vascular patterns within their bodies.

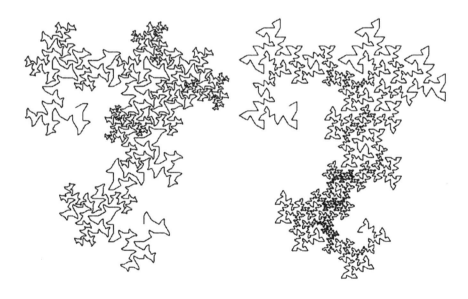

Figure 1.1. Two curves with the same overall shape

Upon returning to your lab on the mainland, you begin studying the hundreds of photographs you took while you were on the island. You can see that many creatures had similar dragon-like bodies, with the same horn-like protrusions, but they were clearly different in their internal details. What accounts for these similarities…and for the differences?

Puzzles abound. In one specific site on the island, you found a large collection of fossils in a cluster. Strangely, their body shapes are very different from each other—having two distinct profiles.

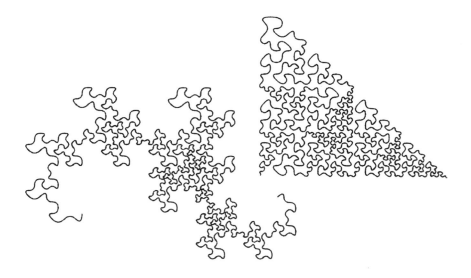

Figure 1.2. Two related curves (splined)

One fossil has a craggy boundary, while the other has a straight boundary. Could it be that they are actually related, but exhibit a different expression of the same common genetic base?

Classification

Like a morphologist attempting to make sense of the varied macrostructures in organisms, we will embark on a similar exploration…with fractal curves. It is as if these curves were natural organisms, uncovered after millions of years in hiding. They are calling out for our analytical eye to classify and organize them into a hierarchy: a *family tree*.

This book sets out to do just that. But unlike Carl Linnaeus in the 1700s, who laid down the foundations of modern taxonomy, we have the benefit of knowing the entire "genetic code" that is responsible for this vast array of forms. In a way, we humans are both the creators and the discoverers of these forms.

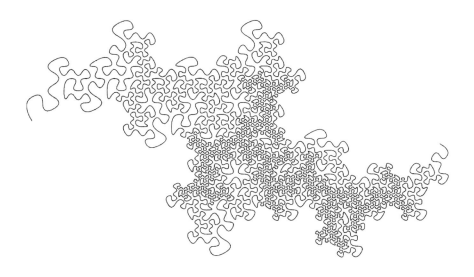

Figure 1.3. A plane-filling curve (splined)

So, you may ask: if we are already able to generate these curves with computer algorithms, shouldn't we therefore know everything there is to know about them? The answer is *no, not entirely*: fractal geometry is not an exercise in making explicit mathematical concepts visible; fractals embody *chaos*. They can be very unpredictable—even when the process of generation is completely deterministic...like the fractal curves in this book.

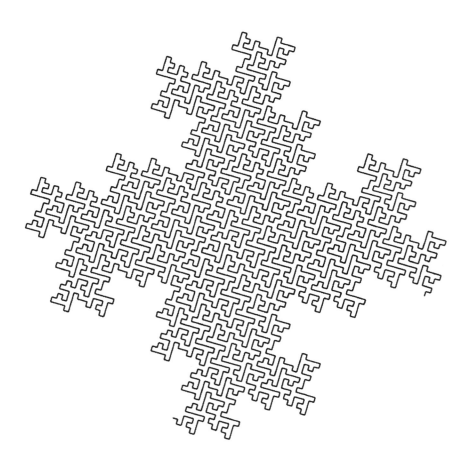

Figure 1.4. Mandelbrot's Quartet

When fractals and chaos theory invaded the clean-edged world of geometry, new perspectives on nature blossomed. With a menagerie of strange beasts that are so complex, so organic, so detailed, we cannot know everything there is to know about them. The archetype of this is the Mandelbrot set [22]: a fractal object first discovered in 1978 that continues to awe and inspire, and will continue to do so as long as we have the computational tools to zoom ever deeper into its remote crevices.

If you happen upon fractal geometry from the viewpoint of visual language and design, you may be inclined to take the perspective of an explorer—applying visual intuition and pattern-finding—and work your way towards a mathematical understanding. That was the impetus for the ideas that eventually came together to form this book. And after more than three decades of exploration and design, a taxonomy has been formulated that places the classic plane-filling curves described in Mandelbrot's *The Fractal Geometry of Nature* [22] (and many more discovered since) under one system.

But a taxonomy is not very useful unless there is an underlying logic for the diversity of shapes being studied; otherwise, it is an arbitrary exercise based on surface appearances. In the case of fractal curves, a question comes to mind: is there a fundamental "nature" behind these forms? In the process of searching for fractal curves that are space-filling and non-overlapping, a consistent logic starts to take shape—calling out for more exploration.

This book describes a taxonomy that includes a large class of plane-filling curves—including the classics. It makes connections between the morphologies of plane-filling curves and concepts from number theory.

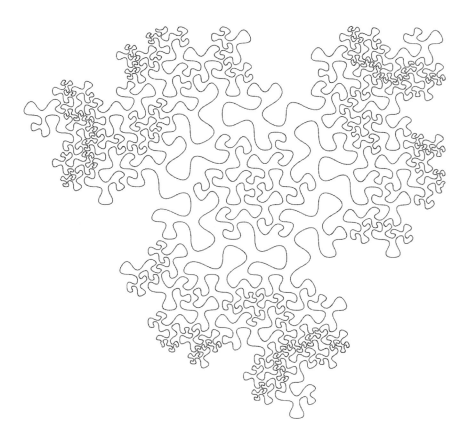

Figure 1.5. A curve of the E(2,1)² family (splined, on a triangular initiator)

A Brief Introduction to Plane-filling Curves

Let's begin with a cursory overview of some basic concepts and approaches to generating fractal curves. This will help to establish some context for describing the taxonomy in the next chapter.

If you magnify a line segment, it still looks straight. If you magnify any portion of a circle, it looks less like a circle and more like a straight line. With a sufficiently deep magnification of any portion of the circle, it appears identical to a straight line. This is a property that lines and circles have in common. Fractal curves do not have this property: they never appear straight—no matter how deep the magnification; fractal curves bend and curl…at *every level of magnification*.

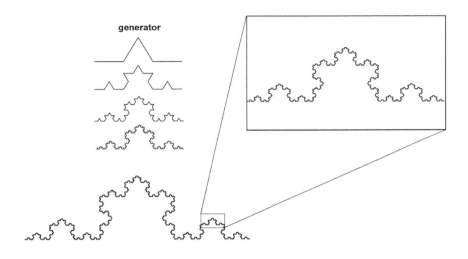

Figure 1.6. The Koch curve magnified to illustrate the concept of infinite detail

The Koch curve (Figure 1.6) is not a plane-filling curve, but it serves as a good example for introducing fractal curves in general. It will appear a few times throughout the book. The figure shows how the Koch curve is constructed, starting with the generator (a shape made of four segments with a triangle-shaped bump in the middle). The first step consists of replacing each of the generator's four segments with a scaled-down copy of the generator. This is called "edge-replacement" (it can also be called, "Koch construction" or "self-substitution"). In the case of the Koch curve, this replacement causes four new smaller bumps to appear on the generator. This process is repeated over and over again. Eventually, the newly-accumulated bumps become so small that we can no longer see them. But the process goes even further: in a true fractal curve, the process is carried on to *infinity*. Thus, every bump, no matter how small, has infinitely many smaller bumps on it.

Every time a new bump is added, the curve grows slightly longer...in fact, in a fractal curve, it becomes *infinitely long* at the limit. This may seem counterintuitive at first, considering that the entire curve—from end to end—occupies a finite space. But the process of iteration is done infinitely many times. This is the key to how fractal curves are able to push their way into a higher dimension.

Fractal Dimension

Figure 1.7 shows three topological types of fractals inserted between the integer dimensions.

Every fractal curve has a fractal dimension (*Hausdorff dimension*) between 1 and 2. A straight line has a fractal dimension of 1. The Koch curve has a fractal dimension of 1.26186. The higher the dimension, the more "space" the curve fills. If a fractal curve doesn't overlap with itself, and if it is so curvy that it essentially visits every point in a planar area, then it is a *plane-filling curve*. It defines a continuous mapping from a lower-dimensional space (a line) into a higher-dimensional space (a plane). Its fractal dimension is 2.

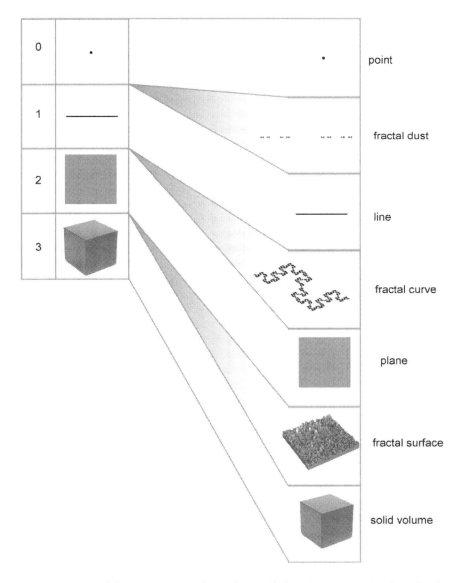

Figure 1.7. Fractals have non-integer dimensions, with fractal curves ranging from 1 to 2

Plane-filling curves that are "self-avoiding" (never touching themselves, and having no contact points) have special properties. As an example of a self-avoiding curve, figure 1.8 shows the process of generating a curve that was discovered in the process of developing this taxonomy. It never touches itself, no matter how densely it fills the shape—even though the final state looks completely filled-in to the eye. But if you were able to magnify it enough, you would see that the lines are still not touching.

Figure 1.8. The first few iterations of the growth of a self-avoiding curve

The angles between the four connected segments in the Koch generator are 60, -120, and 60. Imagine that the Koch curve were made of hinged segments, and you could "squeeze" it so that all the angles change, becoming more acute, which would cause the distance between its endpoints to decrease from 3 down to 2 (Figure 1.9). When the distance reaches 2 it cannot be squeezed any further—there are no gaps left. This squeeze would cause the angles of the generator to become 90, -180, and 90. This curve would not be self-avoiding: it would be maximally-touching.

Figure 1.9. The Koch curve gets squeezed to become the Cesàro Sweep

Figure 1.10 shows a curve derived from the Koch curve created by Wolter Schraa [30]. It shows a continual squeezing of the angles in the Koch curve, causing its fractal dimension to change from 1 to 2 along the extent of the curve. The profile of the Koch curve appears about mid-way in the curve. The right side shows the profile of the Cesàro Sweep, which has a fractal dimension of 2.

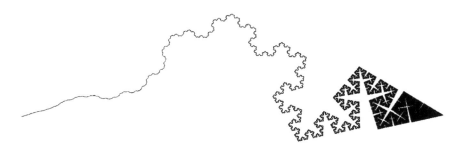

Figure 1.10. A variation of the Koch curve showing the concept of fractal dimension

For explanations of fractal dimension, see Tricot [34], and Kayne [21].

Doodling

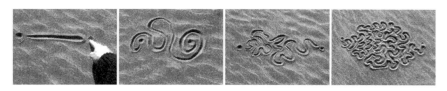

Figure 1.11. Self-avoiding doodles drawn in the sand

A doodling line can be simulated on a computer, using any number of iterative methods—reminiscent of animal foraging paths and other natural processes. A randomly-generated curve has no predictable structure or symmetry—it cannot be described in an elegant or terse way. In this book, the focus is instead on describable emergent structures that arise *deterministically* from relatively simple initial descriptions, and relatively simple rules of growth. There is no randomness, but there is plenty of chaos and complexity.

Infinity vs. Visual Threshold

Anyone can draw a doodle that doesn't overlap or cross itself. But to qualify as a true plane-filling fractal curve, it would have to be infinitely long, drawn with an infinitely-thin pencil, and have infinitely small twists and turns. Even more strange: in order to be completed in finite time, it would have to be drawn at infinite speed.

Although a fractal curve has infinite length and infinite detail at all scales, the special properties of fractals *at the limit* is not central to the taxonomy described in this book. The details that emerge through iterating a generator reach a *visual threshold* when the line segments are so small that they are invisible to the eye—the overall shape is all that can be seen. We are less concerned with what lies beyond a certain threshold—particularly when the nature of that detail remains the same on all levels beyond the macro-scale—due to the curve being self-similar.

Kinds of Fractal Curves

Fractal curves come in many forms, and they arise—sometimes unexpectedly—as a result of many kinds of iterative processes. For comparison, figure 1.12 illustrates a few fractal curves generated using three different methods: (a) approximating the boundaries of sets in the complex plane determined by iterated functions, such as the Mandelbrot set; (b) plotting certain recursive functions along the real number line, such as the Weiertrass function; and (c) constructing curves based on recursive geometrical replacement, such as the Minkowski sausage.

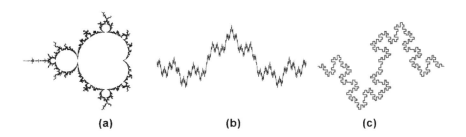

(a)   (b)   (c)

Figure 1.12. Three kinds of fractal curves

19

Edge-replacement is a special kind of recursive geometrical replacement that is specific to line segments (a more general technique being *iterated function systems* [18]). Edge-replacement is based on replacing the segments in a fractal generator with smaller copies of the generator. This is illustrated in Figure 1.13, which shows construction of the Koch curve and the Dragon of Eve [35].

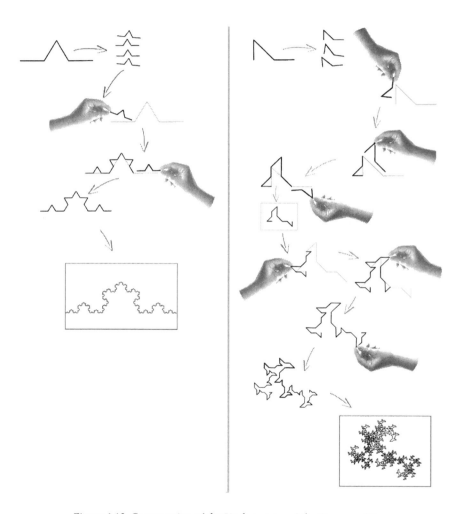

Figure 1.13. Construction of the Koch curve and the Dragon of Eve

Edge-replacement allows copies of the generator to be flipped (rotated by 180 degrees), as demonstrated with the construction of the Dragon of Eve, at the right of Figure 1.13. In some curves, copies of the generator can also be *reflected* about a segment—this will be explained later.

Fractal curves that are constructed in this way are *self-similar*: they exhibit the same features at multiple scales, rotations, and locations.

Teragons

As a curve is generated, it undergoes a progressive increase in detail at each iterative step. The resulting shape is called a "teragon" [22]. In this book, the results at intermediate steps are referred to as "teragon orders." For example, Figure 1.8 shows teragon orders 1-6 (or "teragons 1-6") of a particular curve. "Teragon 0" is simply a line segment.

Edge-Replacement vs Node-Replacement

Edge-replacement is distinct from another technique called "node-replacement" [26]. A popular curve that uses node-replacement is the Hilbert curve [17] (Figure 1.14). (In a later chapter, node-replacement curves will be revisited in terms of their relationship to edge-replacement curves).

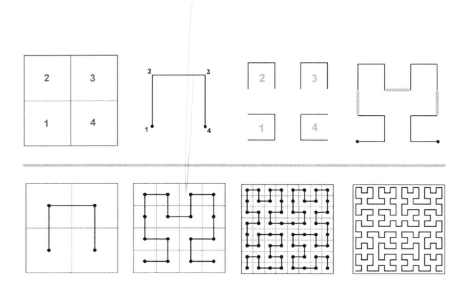

Figure 1.14. Construction of the Hilbert curve

The top-left of Figure 1.14 shows four squares, ordered in a clockwise manner; the centers of these squares are the nodes. To the right of that is the generator, which consists of three lines that connect nodes 1 to 2, 2 to 3, and 3 to 4. Each node is replaced with a scaled-down and rotated copy of the generator. Note that the Hilbert curve (as well as all node-replacement curves) are not strictly self-similar, because at every iteration, a few extra connective segments are required to close the curve (upper-right of Figure 1.14). These segments alter the component shapes that make up the resulting curve at every level.

L-Systems

There are as many algorithms to construct fractal curves as there are creative people in the world who can write code. But most of the algorithms fall into a few common types. One of the most common is

22

L-systems [26], using turtle geometry [1] for drawing lines. Although L-systems are not used to generate the fractal curves in this book, they are important and widely-used, and so the technique will be briefly mentioned here.

In an L-system, a fractal generator is specified as an axiom (a string of symbols). Each symbol can be replaced with other strings, using a set of rules for recursive string rewriting. L-systems encode an entire geometrical transformation process into a one-dimensional string of instructions. Those instructions are fed to a *turtle* (an entity that can rotate in place and move forward, optionally drawing lines as it moves). Figure 1.15 shows how an L-system can be used to construct the Koch curve. Each F is replaced by the string specified in the rule, causing the string to grow to an arbitrary length.

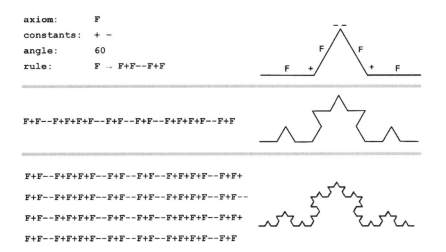

```
axiom:       F
constants:   + -
angle:       60
rule:        F → F+F--F+F
```

```
F+F--F+F+F+F--F+F--F+F--F+F+F+F--F+F
```

```
F+F--F+F+F+F--F+F--F+F--F+F+F+F--F+F+
F+F--F+F+F+F--F+F--F+F--F+F+F+F--F+F--
F+F--F+F+F+F--F+F--F+F--F+F+F+F--F+F+
F+F--F+F+F+F--F+F--F+F--F+F+F+F--F+F
```

Figure 1.15. An L-system for constructing the Koch curve

L-systems are abstract: they are separate from the manner in which the abstract symbols are interpreted into drawing instructions. In contrast, the plane-filling curves described in this book are wedded to a particular space: a lattice of points with algebraic properties. That space has inherent structure within. While it is not as general as an L-system, its inherent structure provides a rich and fertile backdrop for discovering and exploring many properties of plane-filling curves. More abstract is not necessarily better.

Research

The book, *Space-Filling Curves*, by Hans Sagan [29], provides an overview of the classic curves introduced by Hilbert, Sierpinski, Peano, and others, with an emphasis on topology and mathematical analysis. Another book with the same title by Michael Bader [3] explores space-filling curves with emphasis on applications in scientific computing and data processing. These authors are less concerned with the overall shapes of fractal curves, and typically refer to the *square* as the space of interest, describing how a single line can map to that space, as exemplified by the Hilbert curve.

Others have explored various geometrical macro-structures that emerge from iterating over several varieties of fractal generators. Dekking [10] analyzed plane-filling curves in terms of *iterated paper-folding*. Imagine having a thin strip of paper that you can fold any number of times. Each fold increases the number of creases exponentially, as shown in Figure 1.16. The creases are labeled D for *down* and U for *up*. A simple repetitive folding process creates a sequence of turns that—when unfolded to form 90 degree angles—make up a self-similar structure: the Harter-Heighway Dragon curve [9] (abbreviated from now on as "HH Dragon").

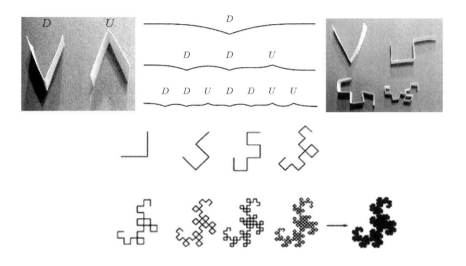

Figure 1.16. Paper-folding to create the HH Dragon curve

The structures that emerge from iterative processes have been studied by many fractal curve explorers, such as McKenna [23], Irving [19], Ryde [28], Karzes [20], Fathauer [11], Fukuda [13], Ventrella, [35], and many others, a few of whom will be mentioned later in the book. The list of fractal curve explorers is growing; it would not be possible to credit all of them in this book.

The Lattice

Curves with low fractal dimension (close to 1) are *almost* straight. They have plenty of room to wander around with little risk of bumping into their own paths. Higher-dimensioned curves are more susceptible to self-collision. At dimensions close to 2, it becomes necessary to use a lattice (or a grid) as a guide to avoid a complete mess (the reason for this will become more apparent in the next chapter). When searching for new plane-filling fractal curves, confining the search to a lattice is therefore very useful, as demonstrated by McKenna [23] and also by Arndt [2], who reveals novel curves in various grids, using L-systems.

Complex integers (introduced in the next chapter) provide a lattice framework, and they also happen to be rich in terms of number theory. Several techniques for generating a variety of fractal structures using complex integers have been studied by Gilbert [14], and Stange [31]. Complex integers can also be used as a framework for studying (and generating) plane-filling fractal curves.

This brings us to a core theme in the book: a lattice-based framework for categorizing edge-replacement plane-filling fractal curves, and its relationship to complex integers. Much of the inspiration for placing fractal curves in a complex integer framework is based on suggestions by Adam Goucher [15].

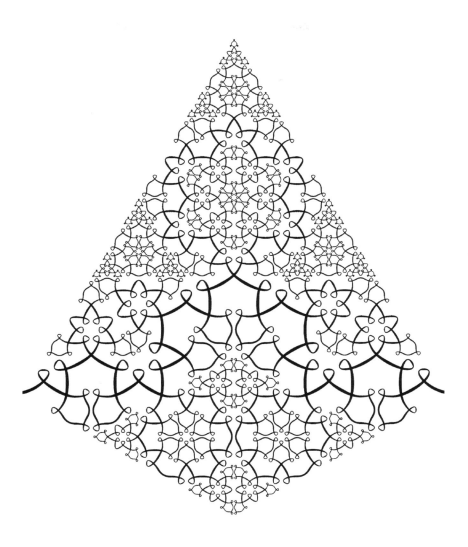

Figure 1.17. A self-crossing curve of the E(3,0) family (splined)

2

Taxonomy

We have now arrived at the core theme in this book: a taxonomy representing all plane-filling curves using edge-replacement. (For brevity, these will be referred to as "curves" throughout the book). It will be necessary to delve into some technical details and definitions before a bigger picture can take shape. You can always choose to skip ahead and study the illustrations throughout the book—to build intuition using the powers of your visual cortex. If you do, please come back to this chapter, as it presents key terms and concepts.

All biological organisms are classified within a taxonomy of eight ranks: domain, kingdom, phylum, class, order, family, genus, and species. The five ranks in the taxonomy of fractal curves described in this book are not related to the taxonomy of biological organisms. However, it is intentional that the fractal curve ranks are ordered from the most general to the most specific:

1. Domain   (square (Gaussian) or triangular (Eisenstein) lattice)
2. Root   (the origin of a series of families)
3. Family   (a class of curves based on the root)
4. Generator (the seed for generating a curve in a family)
5. Transforms (rotations and reflections applied to the generator)

The hierarchy of these ranks is shown in a cartoon schematic in Figure 2.1.

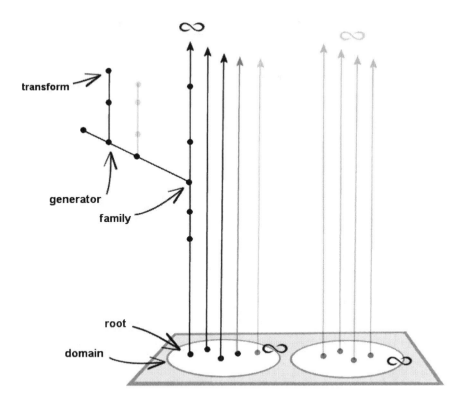

Figure 2.1. A cartoon schematic showing the hierarchy of fractal curve ranks

These five ranks are explained below.

1. Domain

Complex numbers have two parts: *real* and *imaginary*. The entire set of complex numbers fills the *complex plane*. It maps to a Cartesian grid, and it is infinitely dense. A subset of the complex plane—the *Gaussian integers*—forms a square lattice: a regular grid of points arranged orthogonally. A Gaussian integer is defined as a complex number whose real and imaginary parts are both integers. The sum, difference, or product of any two Gaussian integers is always another Gaussian integer: thus, the Gaussian integers are *closed* under addition and multiplication.

In this book we will also include the *Eisenstein integers* in our definition of "complex integer"; the Eisenstein integers form a triangular lattice (explained later). They are also closed under addition and multiplication. The Gaussian and Eisenstein integers both form *Euclidean domains:* the fundamental theorem of arithmetic can be applied. The taxonomy described in this book is based on these two Euclidean domains. Figure 2.2 shows the Gaussian domain (G), which forms a square lattice, and the Eisenstein domain (E), which forms a triangular lattice (sometimes it is called a "hexagonal lattice", referring to the lattice points as the centers of hexagons).

Figure 2.2. Gaussian and Eisenstein integer lattices

When we talk about integers, we are usually referring to the *rational integers*: those familiar evenly-spaced points that lie on the one-dimensional real number line. The complex integers occupy the plane, and thus have more geometric symmetry than the rational integers. Throughout this book, the word "integer" will typically be used in reference to complex integers.

Transform to Eisenstein

Complex numbers are normally expressed in the form a+bi, where a is the real part and b is the imaginary part (i denotes *imaginary*). Since Eisenstein integers do not line up orthogonally, they require extra specification, and are typically expressed in the form a+bw, where a and b are integers, and $w = (-1+i\sqrt{3})/2$. Think of this as a mapping from the square lattice to the triangular lattice. To illustrate this, Figure 2.3 shows a mapping from a unique Gaussian integer G(2,1) to a unique Eisenstein integer E(2,1). It is shifted leftward and downward, while the other integers are unchanged because they lie on the real axis.

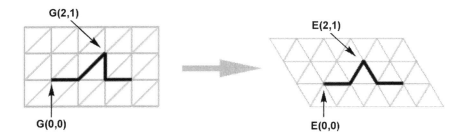

Figure 2.3. Mapping of integer (2,1) from Gaussian to Eisenstein

The shift to these components (a, b) can be expressed as follows:
a-shifted = a - b/2;
b-shifted = b * $\sqrt{3}$/2.

Abbreviated Notation

In this book, complex integers are expressed using the simplified form (a,b)—a notation typically used to specify Cartesian coordinates. It is made explicit when the domain is Gaussian vs. Eisenstein. For instance, "E(2,5)" specifies the Eisenstein integer $2+5w$, and "G(-2, -1)" specifies the Gaussian integer $-2-1i$.

Norm

The distance of a complex number from the origin (0,0) can be calculated using the Pythagorean theorem. This is called the "Euclidian distance." Squaring that number results in what is called the "norm."

For complex integers, the norm is always a positive rational integer.

(The term "norm" is sometimes used to refer to the Euclidean distance, but that will not be used in this context).

As an example, the Euclidean distance of G(1,1) from the origin is the square root of 2 (the diagonal of a unit square). Since that number squared is 2, the norm of G(1,1) is 2.

Slices

The Gaussian Integer lattice can be divided into eight pie slices (octants) that are equal except for the isometric transformations of rotation and reflection. Similarly, the Eisenstein Integer lattice can be divided into twelve slices (Figure 2.4). Given this isometry, we can ignore all but one slice for the purposes of this taxonomy; we will only refer to the slice that lies above and adjacent to the positive real axis (shown as gray in the figure). These slices will be referenced often throughout the book.

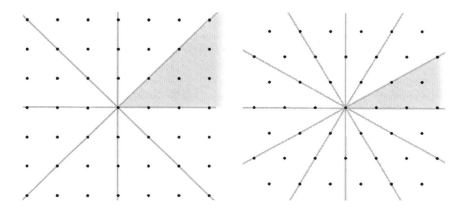

Figure 2.4. Referenced slices of the Gaussian and Eisenstein integers

Figure 2.5 shows some small norms in the Gaussian and Eisenstein domains.

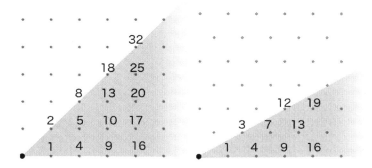

Figure 2.5. Norms in the Gaussian and Eisenstein domains

Complex Multiplication

Students of math are often confused when they first learn about complex numbers, because they are typically confronted with the counterintuitive concept of the square root of -1. This confusion is unnecessary if the goal is to gain a procedural understanding of the behaviors of complex numbers in the plane. In this book, *i* is not used at all. The only knowledge needed in this context is a basic understanding of complex addition and multiplication (and *conjugation* —a reflection about the real axis).

Complex addition is accomplished by simply adding the real parts and the imaginary parts separately; it is the same as adding two vectors. Multiplication is key to understanding the magical powers of complex numbers. It is achieved through a particular "mixing" of the real and imaginary components of the factors to construct the real and imaginary parts of the product. Figure 2.6 shows how the integer (a,b) is multiplied by the integer (c,d) to create the real and imaginary parts of the resulting product. Complex multiplication can be thought of as a rotation and a dilation relative to the origin (an idea that will be revisited later).

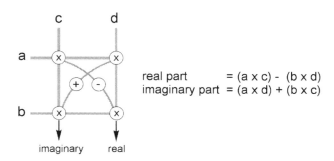

real part $\quad$ = (a x c) - (b x d)
imaginary part = (a x d) + (b x c)

Figure 2.6. Complex multiplication

2. Root

A "root" is defined here as an integer that is *not* a perfect power. It cannot be expressed in the form x^n, where x has norm > 1 and where n is a rational integer > 1. The set of rational integers with this property is described in the On-line Encyclopedia of Integer Sequences at the web site: http://oeis.org/A007916 . This integer set is not given a name. So, for the present context, we will call it the set of "roots".

For illustration, consider the first 18 natural numbers:

1	**2**	**3**	4	**5**	**6**	**7**	8	9
10	**11**	**12**	**13**	**14**	**15**	16	**17**	**18**

The roots are shown in bold-black, and the perfect powers are shown in light-gray. Note that the numbers 4, 8, and 16 are powers of the root 2, and 9 is a power of the root 3.

Roots are primitive building blocks analogous to *primes*, except that instead of being primitives of *multiplication*, they are primitives of *exponentiation*.

Let's look at an example in the rational integers. The rational integer 125 is not a root: it is a perfect power, because it can be expressed in the form x^n ($5^3 = 125$). Likewise, 25 is not a root: it is a perfect power, because it can be expressed in the form x^n ($5^2 = 25$). But the number 5 is a root, since it has no integer roots of its own (other than itself, as 5^1). No integer multiplied by itself n times equals 5.

All primes are roots, but not all roots are primes. For instance, the rational integer 10 is a root but it is not a prime: it is a root because no integer multiplied by itself n times equals 10. It is not a prime because 10 is the product of 2 and 5.

The same definition can be applied to the complex integers: both domains have an infinite number of roots. They can be shown visually as a subset of points lying on the lattice. Three roots in each domain are shown—with norms—in Figure 2.7. In the Gaussian domain, they are (1,1), (2, 1), and (3, 0), having norms 2, 5, and 9. In the Eisenstein domain, they are (2, 1), (2, 0), and (3, 1), having norms 3, 4 and 7.

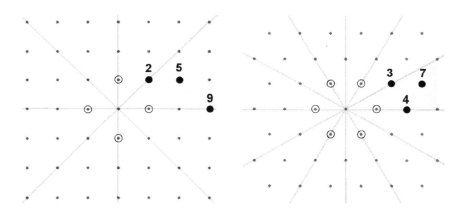

Figure 2.7. Some roots (with norms shown) in the Gaussian and Eisenstein domains

The significance of roots will be made apparent soon.

Units

Figure 2.7 also shows the *units* (the dotted circles surrounding the origin). These have norm 1.

Any rational integer multiplied by -1 keeps its magnitude and gets reflected to the opposite (positive or negative) side of the number line. Similarly, any complex integer multiplied by a unit will keep the same magnitude (and norm), and will optionally rotate about the origin. The units are not associated with any fractal curves; only the integers with norms greater than 1 have associated curves, and each integer represents a family of curves. This will become more clear when we consider the set of perfect powers that grow out of roots through exponentiation…which brings us to the concept of a *family set*.

Family Set

Power laws are important to fractals; they express self-similarity. The relationships among families of curves can also be described in terms of power laws. Consider the set of perfect powers of a root among the rational integers. For example, take the first five powers of the root 2:

$$2^1 = 2; \qquad 2^2 = 4; \qquad 2^3 = 8; \qquad 2^4 = 16; \qquad 2^5 = 32;$$

A 2D analog of this series can be generated as the powers of the Gaussian integer (1,1), using complex number multiplication:

$(1,1)^1 = (1,1)$ *norm = 2*

$(1,1)^2 = (0,2)$ *norm = 4*

$(1,1)^3 = (-2,2)$ *norm = 8*

$(1,1)^4 = (-4,0)$ *norm = 16*

$(1,1)^5 = (-4, -4)$ *norm = 32*

These Gaussian integers are plotted in Figure 2.8. The norms are labeled along the spiral.

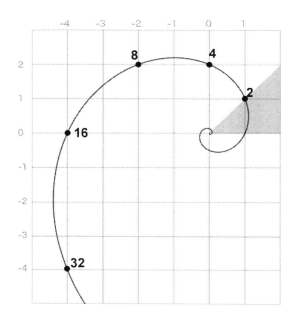

Figure 2.8. The G(1,1) family set lies on a power-of-2 spiral

Starting from any root, we can generate a family set by calculating the consecutive integer powers of the root.

Family sets are *mutually disjoint,* and the union of all family sets comprises the entire set of integers greater than norm 1. Using this categorization scheme ensures that *all* fractal curve families are taken into account.

A family set can be referenced by its root. For instance, "the family set of E(2,1)" refers to $E(2,1)^n$ for all $n > 0$.

Most family sets lie on logarithmic spirals, but some of them lie on straight lines (on the positive real axis), as shown in Figure 2.9. In this figure, four family sets are shown originating from roots with norms 2, 5, 9, and 10, shown in white circles.

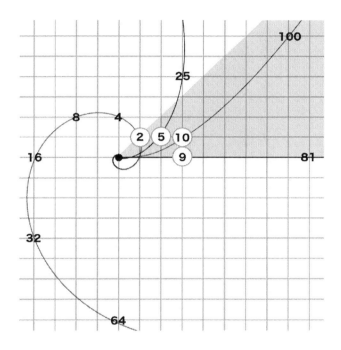

Figure 2.9. Four family sets in the Gaussian domain, showing norms

The family sets in Figure 2.9 show the following norms (in bold-font) below. The roots are shown in the left column.

2	4	8	16	32	64	128	...
5	25	125	635	3125	...		
9	81	729	6561	...			
10	100	1000	...				

So that all operations can be done within the gray slice, we will assume that any integers lying outside of the slice are mapped to it by way of reflections and rotations. As an example, Figure 2.10 shows how the $G(1,1)^n$ family set gets mapped into the gray slice, causing its associated power-of-two spiral to zigzag through the slice.

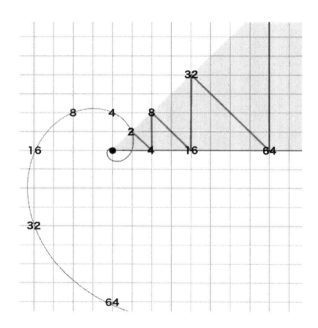

Figure 2.10. The $G(1,1)^n$ family set remapped to the gray slice

Primes

Similar to a rational integer prime—which is only divisible by 1 and itself—a prime p in the Gaussian or Eisenstein domain is only divisible by a unit and one of its *associates* (that is: an integer with the same norm as p that is the product of p and a unit). The integer p cannot be written as the product of two integers that *both* have a smaller norm than p. Later we will take a look at some primes and their associated families.

3. Family

A family is simply one of the integers existing in the family set. Every family set has an infinite number of families, starting at the root (the "root family"), and progressing through the family set (the "power families").

A family can be identified as a power of its root (e.g., $E(2,1)^3$), with the exponent representing its *order* within the family set. Alternatively, it can be identified by its exact integer components (e.g., $E(3,6)$). In some cases, a family can be referenced simply by its norm, although multiple families can have the same norm. For example, the Eisenstein families $E(3,1)$ and $E(3,2)$ both have norm 7, as shown in Figure 2.11. They are reflections of each other (reflected about the line separating the gray slice from the one above it). (There are in fact 12 Eisenstein integers in all with norm 7, if you include all 12 slices of the plane).

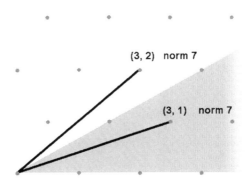

Figure 2.11. Two families with norm 7

There can also be families that have the same norm *but they are not reflections of each other* (such as G(3,4) and G(5,0), both having norm 25 —these will be visited later).

Tree Diagram

The ranks described so far (*domain, root,* and *family*) are used to classify every family within the hierarchy. Each family is associated with a unique integer in the first (gray) slice of the complex plane. This hierarchical structure can also be visualized with a tree diagram (Figure 2.12).

The trunk of the tree represents all plane-filling curves that can be generated using edge-replacement. The trunk splits off into two branches: the Gaussian domain and the Eisenstein domain.

Each domain then splits off into an infinite number of branches representing the roots. A few of the smallest roots are shown, and the branch with the infinity symbol implies that there are infinitely more roots.

Each root in turn branches off into its family set. There are infinitely many families in a family set, as indicated by the symbol r^n. For each family shown, there is a representative curve at the end of the branch.

Finally, the norm of the family is shown at the perimeter.

Figure 2.12. A tree diagram illustrating the classification of curve families

4. Generator

The last two ranks (*generator* and *transform*) specify the genetic code of each individual curve within a family.

To understand a fractal curve generator, think of all the ways you can walk along a lattice. Consider the Eisenstein family at integer E(2,1), which is the dot labeled "3" we saw earlier in Figure 2.7. Its norm is 3. Figure 2.13 shows six paths starting from the origin (0,0)—denoted as A, and ending on the family integer E(2,1)—denoted as B, given exactly three unit steps.

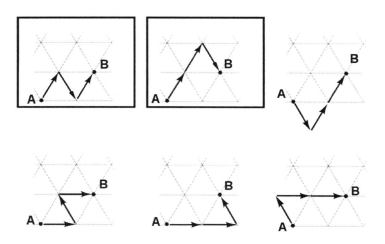

Figure 2.13. Six ways to walk a triangular lattice in three unit steps from A to B

In the figure, the first two paths are framed with black boxes, indicating that they are unique. The other four paths can be described as isometric transformations of the first two.

The number of steps (connected segments) in these paths is 3, which is the same as the family norm. Consider each path as a summation of three units in the Eisenstein domain. It demonstrates that there is more than one way to say "1+1+1" in the complex plane. This path is called the *generator*. The first two generators in Figure 2.13 can be represented as three integers in the Eisenstein domain:

Generator 1:   (1, 1), (0, -1), (1, 1)
Generator 2:   (1, 1), (1, 1), (0, -1)

(Remember from Figure 2.3 that in the Eisenstein domain the specified integers are transformed (using w) so that they conform to the triangular lattice).

Fractal Generator as Array of Complex Integers
Every fractal generator described in this book can be understood as an array of complex integers. And if the generator determines a plane-filling curve, then…

the sum of these integers is equal to the family integer.

Similarly, the sum of the *norms* of the integers is equal to the *norm* of the family integer. This can be expressed in a way that is related to the fractal (Hausdorff) dimension of a fractal curve. The equation $D = \log(N)/\log(r)$ can be used to calculate the fractal dimension D of a curve, where N equals the number of segments in the fractal generator (assuming that each segment has length 1), and where r is the distance between the endpoints of the generator.

A commonly-used example is the Koch curve, which has 4 segments of length 1 in its generator (N=4), and its generator spans a length of 3 (r=3). So for the Koch curve, D = log(4)/log(3) = 1.26186.

Figure 2.14 shows the Koch curve along with three other curves of the E(3,0) family. It illustrates an exploration that is similar to one made previously by McKenna, who tested variations of the Koch curve in a triangular grid. Specifically, he was searching for curves confined to a triangle with sides of length 3, tiled with 9 sub-triangles [23].

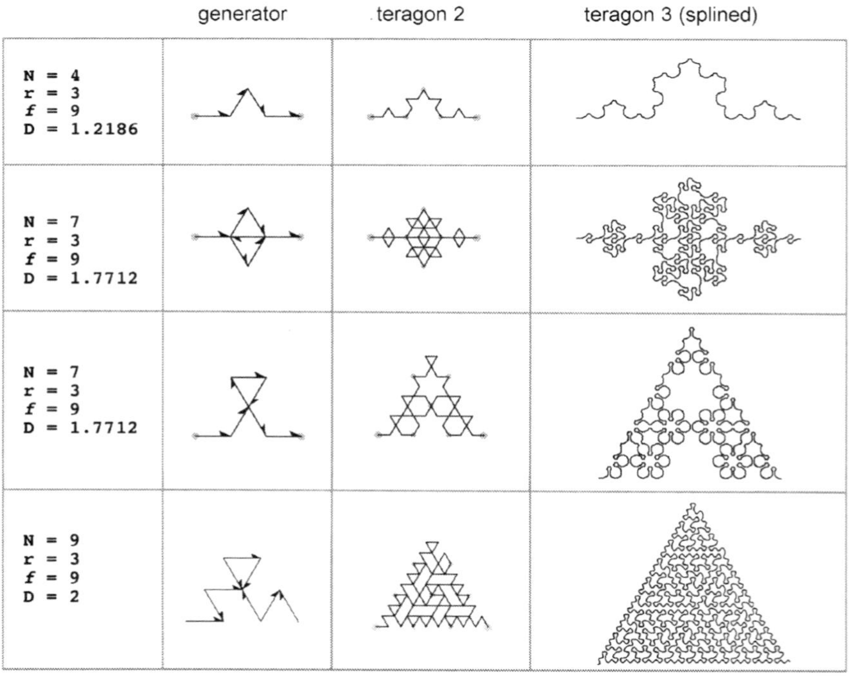

	generator	teragon 2	teragon 3 (splined)
N = 4 r = 3 f = 9 D = 1.2186			
N = 7 r = 3 f = 9 D = 1.7712			
N = 7 r = 3 f = 9 D = 1.7712			
N = 9 r = 3 f = 9 D = 2			

Figure 2.14. Relatives of the Koch curve in the E(3,0) family.

For each curve, N and r are shown, along with the family norm f and fractal dimension D. In this taxonomy, the sum of the norms of the integers in the generator is equal to N, and the family norm f is equal to r^2. Thus, for any plane-filling curve represented in this taxonomy…

$$N = f = r^2.$$

Mixed-Norm Generators, Divisors, and Power Laws

The generators in Figure 2.14 each consist of integers that are units: their norms are all 1. An important point to introduce now is that many of the fascinating curves shown in this book are based on mixed-norm generators; their teragons have segments of varying lengths. These generators belong to the *power families*, which are all of the families in a family set except for the root family. Power families have curves with integers that can be either units or powers of the family root. This is related to the fact that fractal self-similarity obeys power laws.

Consider a Gaussian integer with norm 4. There are four Gaussian integers that have a norm of 4: (2,0), (-2,0), (0,2), and (0,-2), shown as the white circles in Figure 2.15. The four roots of these integers: (1,1), (-1,1), (-1,-1), (1,-1) each have norm 2. Included are the four units: (1,0), (-1,0), (0,1), (0,-1). All the roots are shown as black dots. They have lines connecting them to the origin. It's important to notice that the integers with norm 2 are connected with diagonal lines.

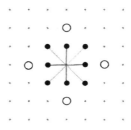

Figure 2.15. Divisors (black dots) of Gaussian integers with norm 4 (white dots)

How many ways can these integers be added up so that their sums equal a Gaussian integer with norm 4? (Let's consider only one integer with norm 4—namely, (2,0)—since the other three are equal, except for the isometric transformations of rotation and reflection). One way to answer this question is with a picture:

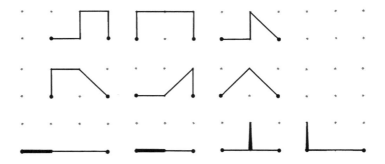

Figure 2.16. Ten ways to add Gaussian integers that sum to (2,0)

In Figure 2.16, the four sums illustrated at the bottom have overlapping line segments, which make them appear to have only three segments.

All fractal curve generators of a common family have integers that sum to the same integer (specifically, the *family integer*). But not any set of integers that sum to the family integer can be used as a generator that determines a plane-filling curve. For instance, consider a Gaussian integer of norm 5, such as G(2,1). It can be described as the sum of various permutations of Gaussian integers with norms 1, 2, and 4 (note that there is no such thing as a Gaussian integer with norm 3). Just a few of the many permutations are shown in Figure 2.17.

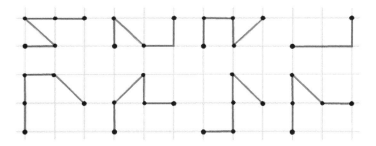

Figure 2.17. A few permutations of integers with norms 1, 2, and 4 that sum to norm 5

None of these can be used as generators to make plane-filling curves. The reason is that Gaussian integers with norm 5 are *prime*; integers with norms 2 and 4 are not divisors of integers with norm 5. Only units are divisors in prime families. All of the integers in a generator must be divisors of the family integer. Furthermore, if the family integer is a perfect power, then those integers must be *roots* of the family integer.

In terms of combinations of integer norms, all generators fall into the following categories:

1. *root* (the family integer is not a perfect power)

      a. *prime* (generator integers are units only)

      b. *composite* (generator integers may not all be units)

2. *power* (generator integers are roots of a power family integer)

Prime families are root families whose generators only have integers of norm 1 (units). Generators of power families can have integers with a combination of norms (as long as they are all roots of the family integer). Note also that the divisors of power family integers are all powers of the family root; they are perfect powers.

Primes, Composites, and Powers

Figure 2.18, shows four generators with associated teragons. At the top-left is a generator of the prime family G(3,2) with norm 13 (all integers have norm 1). It was discovered in the process of developing this taxonomy—and described previously by McKenna [23]—it will be revisited later. At the top-right is a generator of the composite root family E(4,2) with norm 12 (all integers have norm 3, and they are all divisors of 12). At the bottom-left is a generator of the power family E(3,0) with norm 9 (the integers have norms 1 and 3). At the bottom-right is a generator of the power family E(4,0) with norm 16 (the integers have norms 1 and 4). It is the generator for the Tsunami Curve —illustrated at the beginning of the book.

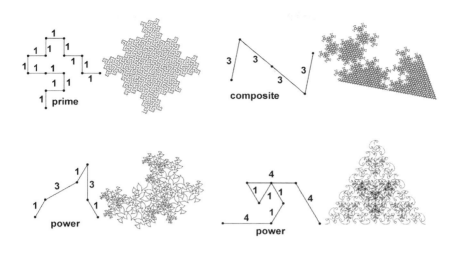

Figure 2.18. Generators with varying sized norms, with associated teragons

Why must these generators only include divisors of the family integer? And why should generators with integers having varying norms only include integers that are powers of the family root? These rules may appear arbitrary at first, but the rationale should become clearer as we go. The fundamental principle at play here is that fractal self-similarity obeys power laws.

What would happen if we attempted to break the rule by taking the upper-left generator and replacing the 4th and 5th integers with a single integer having norm 4? We know that 4 is not a divisor of 13, so we have a hint that there could be trouble ahead. This norm-4 integer is illustrated as the dark line in Figure 2.19a. Figure 2.19b shows how each integer is associated with a square area, shown as a gray square adjacent to the integer's line segment. This association is indicated by a short line perpendicular to the line segment (this kind of association is explained later in the section on *transforms*). The large square associated with the norm 4 integer is shown in dark-gray.

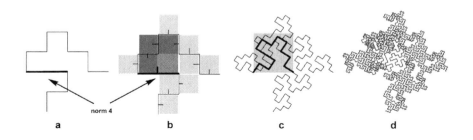

Figure 2.19. Experimental variation of the G(3,2) curve from Figure 2.18

We can see that overlapping areas and tremas (holes) begin to appear in the next two teragons, shown in (c) and (d). The same problem would occur if this larger square were oriented downward instead of upward. There appears to be no way to copy the generator onto this segment without causing a mess.

With this taxonomy, the sum of the integers in a generator must be equal to the family integer. The experimental variation just described has a sum of 15. Notice that there is no such thing as a Gaussian integer with norm 15. (The norm of a Gaussian integer is always the sum of two squares). Both experimentation and number theory support the rationale for this rule.

A similar experiment is shown in Figure 2.20. It is a variation of the Tsunami curve we just saw at the bottom-right of Figure 2.18. If we were to replace each of the three integers having norm 4 with two integers having norm 1, then we would end up with a total of 10 integers of norm 1, and the sum of the norms would go from 16 down to 10. Does there exist a plane-filling curve in the Eisenstein domain with norm 10? The gray triangles in Figure 2.20b may give a clue to the answer. The first four teragons of this curve are shown in Figure 2.20c with splined (curved) rendering. The result is interesting, but it is not plane-filling; the family integer has norm 16 but the sum of the generator's integers has a norm of 10, so its fractal dimension is less than 2.

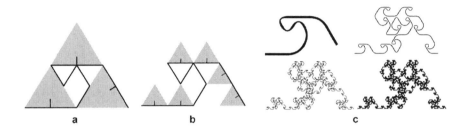

Figure 2.20. Variation of the Tsunami curve from Figure 2.18

Emergent Morphology

Now let's return to the six generators shown at the top of Figure 2.16. These generators are responsible for the wonderful variety of shapes in Figure 2.21.

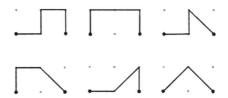

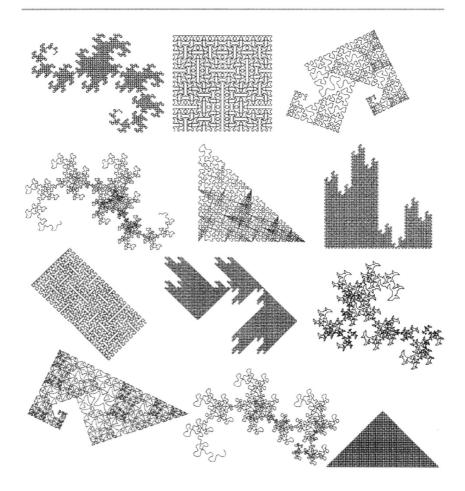

Figure 2.21. The 6 generator shapes and 12 unique curves of the G(2,0) family

How is it that such variety can emerge from these simple generators? The key lies in some special attributes that determine the *transform*— the final rank in the taxonomy.

5. Transform

When explaining edge-replacement, we say that each segment in the generator is replaced with a small copy of the generator. (Fractal curve algorithms can use many methods to achieve the same effect). You could think of each copy as being transformed from the coordinate space of the generator to the coordinate space of the segment—which requires a translation, a rotation, and a scaling < 1. But there are additional transforms that can take place within the space of the segment.

Imagine a strand of DNA that encodes for some aspect of a body plan being read backwards or upside-down. Let's bring back our friend the Koch curve. Consider what happens if the instructions for drawing the Koch curve specified that the last segment be *reflected* so that it is upside-down. This can be illustrated with a turtle shown from the side-view (Figure 2.22).

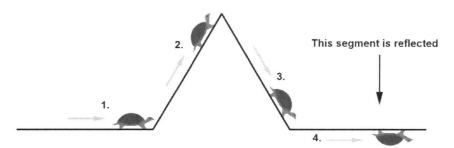

Figure 2.22. The Koch curve generator with its last segment reflected

This reflection makes its influence on teragon 2, showing up as a downward bump in the last fourth of the curve (Figure 2.23).

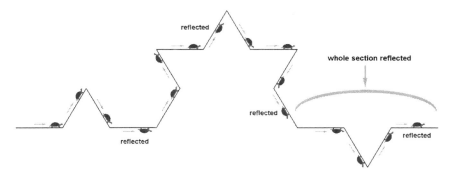

Figure 2.23. Second teragon of the Koch curve generator with its last segment reflected

Notice how the reflection of the 16th segment has been *re-reflected*, putting the turtle upright again! This alternation of reflections continues each time the teragon is iterated. Figure 2.24. shows the result after iterating to teragon 4.

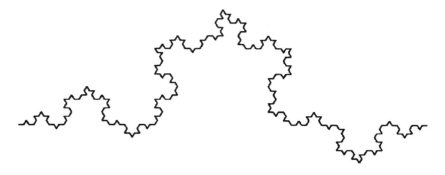

Figure 2.24. Fourth teragon from Koch curve generator with its last segment reflected

Seeing the effect of a reflected segment in the Koch curve may not be very interesting. But it becomes more interesting (in fact, critical) when we see how transforming segments allows many plane-filling curves to be possible—and in particular, the self-avoiding ones. Consider the generator in Figure 2.25, which has no transforms. Teragons 1-6 are shown.

Figure 2.25. A generator with no transforms that creates messy teragons

Next, consider what happens if the second and fourth segments are reflected (Figure 2.26).

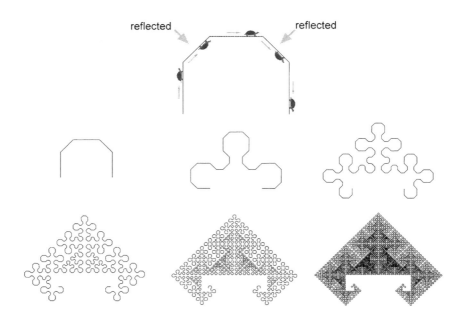

Figure 2.26. The same generator with alternating reflections

By simply reflecting these two segments, the resulting curve avoids self-contact.

Description of Transforms

We have just seen the effect of reflecting segments. But the encoding for a transform on a segment actually has two components, which are both binary: *rotation* and *reflection*. The rotation component consists of a full 180-degree rotation about the center of the segment (for clarity, let's call this a "180-rotation").

In the process of constructing transformed copies of the generator, a 180-rotation can be achieved by reading the generator's integers and associated transforms *backwards*.

A reflection can be achieved with two complex number operations: (1) taking the conjugate of the generator (its mirror-image on the opposite side of the real axis), and (2) assuming the family integer does not already lie on the real axis, multiplying the generator by the unit G(0,1) or E(0,1) to rotate it back to its axis of reflection. Figure 2.27 illustrates these operations as applied to the generator shown in Figure 2.26. (Although the generator is shown oriented upright in Figure 2.26, its natural pose is at a 45 degree angle, because it is in fact a member of the G(2,2) family).

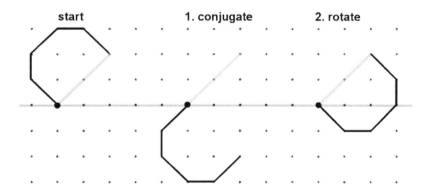

Figure 2.27. Two operations are used to reflect a generator about its family integer

(Not all generators permit reflections, as explained later).

Visualizing Transforms

The chart in Figure 2.28 shows alternate visual representations for the four possible transforms, given all combinations of 180-rotations and reflections. These visual representations will be used in several illustrations throughout the book.

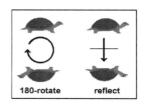

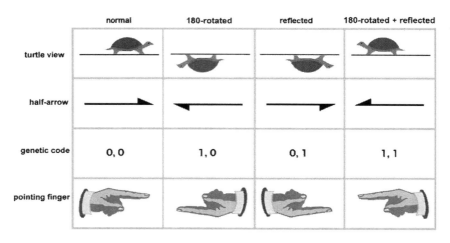

Figure 2.28. Representations for transforms

The generator for the Dragon of Eve is shown in Figure 2.29, demonstrating all four possible transforms.

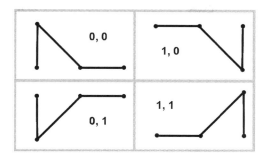

Figure 2.29. All possible transforms applied to the Dragon of Eve generator

Note that a 180-rotation produces the same effect as two orthogonal reflections (one about the segment and one about a *perpendicular that bisects the segment*). This representation would work easily as well, and it is simpler in some ways, since all four transformations can be considered as combinations of these two reflections. In fact, this was used in a previous version of the taxonomy [35]. However, the 180-rotation operation has particular salience in the context of lattice symmetry, and it can be used on any generator segment, while the reflection operation only works for families that lie on an axis of reflection (as explained later in the section on axis-aligned curves). With this in mind, the representation was changed from two orthogonal reflections to a rotation plus a reflection.

The Dragon of Eve generator can produce very different curves if alternate segments are 180-rotated. Figure 2.30 shows how 180-rotating the last segment of the generator determines the Dragon of Eve, while 180-rotating the middle segment creates a curve with intricate tiling patterns.

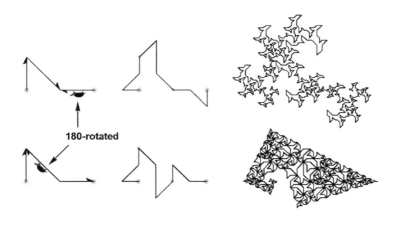

Figure 2.30. The Dragon of Eve and a close relative

Figure 2.31 shows an example a self-avoiding curve of the E(3,0) family that uses every combination of 180-rotations and reflections to stay out of its own way.

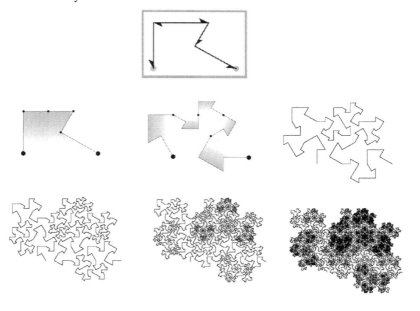

Figure 2.31. A self-avoiding curve of the E(3,0) family with self-avoiding transforms

The transforms for the segments of its generator are expressed as five pairs of bits:

(1, 1), (1, 0), (0, 0), (0, 0), (0, 1).

These transforms are illustrated with half arrows in the generator.

The generator for the classic HH Dragon curve requires a (1, 0) transform in one of its two segments. Figure 2.32 shows a generator with the second segment 180-rotated, along with an associated teragon.

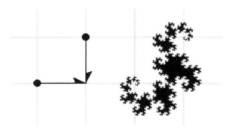

Figure 2.32. HH Dragon generator and a high-order teragon

The HH Dragon generator has only two segments. You may be wondering: what is the result of applying some other transforms on this 2-segment generator? Figure 2.33 shows three variations of transforms.

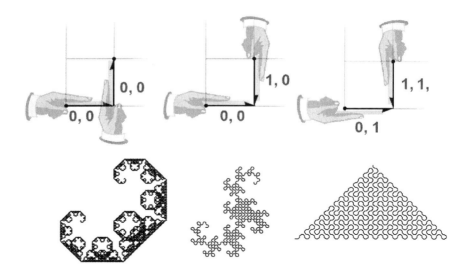

Figure 2.33. Transforms for the Lévy C curve, the HH Dragon, and the Pólya curve

When no transforms are used, the Lévy C curve results (left). This curve crosses and overlaps itself in a complicated way. The other two transforms result in two plane-filling curves (the only two in the G(1,1) family: the HH Dragon curve and the Pólya curve). But there are more transforms that can be applied to this generator. Figure 2.34 shows all 16 possible transforms.

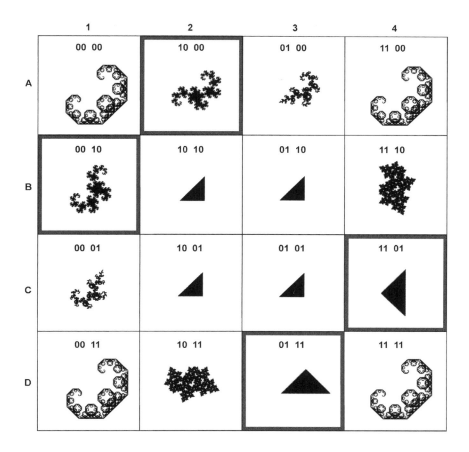

Figure 2.34. Curves resulting from every possible transform of the G(1,1) generator

In this figure, two transforms determine the HH dragon; they are highlighted with squares in positions A2 and B1. Positions C4 and D3 show the two transforms that determine the Pólya curve. These curves are "well-behaved", while the other curves either cross or overlap with themselves. The four curves in the middle are instances of the Cesàro Sweep (which has two variations, shown later in the G(1,1) and $G(1,1)^2$ families).

Now let's return to the first two paths shown in Figure 2.13. They represent the generators of the E(2,1) family, with norm 3. Given all possible permutations of transforms, how many admit plane-filling curves? The answer is 10 (Figure 2.35).

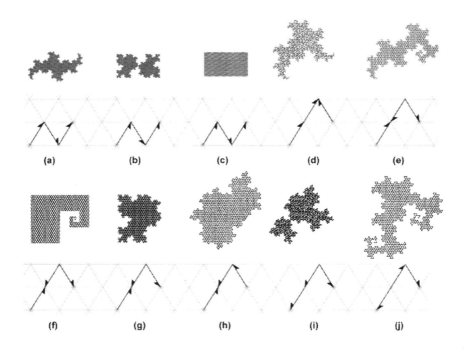

Figure 2.35. The 10 curves of the E(2,1) family, shown with generators

Curve (a) is the Terdragon. It has no transforms. Curve (b) is the result of reflecting all 3 segments of the Terdragon. Curve (d) is the "Fractal Chair" [4]. Curve (e) is the "Half-Terdragon" [20]. Curve (j) is the "Walking Terdragon" [36]. Curves (h) and (j) are both self-avoiding.

Curve (c) is the result of reflecting the first and third segments of the Terdragon (Figure 2.36, lower-right). Note that the first and third segments have been reflected in the Terdragon generator to determine this curve. These reflections are shown with dark lines in the middle of the figure. Haverkort [16] made the observation that this curve is basically a stretched version of the original Peano curve [25].

Figure 2.36. Ter Dragon and a transformed version similar to the original Peano curve

What would happen if 180-rotations had been used instead of reflections? The answer is…*nothing*, because this generator has point-symmetry about its center: it is identical to itself when rotated 180-degrees.

The symmetry of a generator determines how it can be transformed in the lattice. For instance, consider the generator for the 5-Dragon (Figure 2.37). Like the Terdragon generator, it has point-symmetry, and so a 180-rotation has no effect. But unlike the Terdragon generator, it cannot be reflected, because that would break it out of the lattice, as shown at bottom-right.

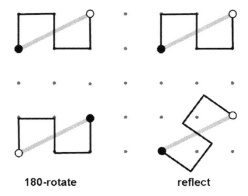

180-rotate   reflect

Figure 2.37. 5-Dragon generator demonstrates how G(2,1) curves do not allow reflections

This point will be revisited later when we explore a variation of the 5-Dragon in the G(5,0) family.

Transforming segments appears to be a necessary ingredient for generating self-avoiding curves, as exemplified by the two curves in Figure 2.38. (Notice how different transforms are applied to the same generator, resulting in subtle differences in their teragons).

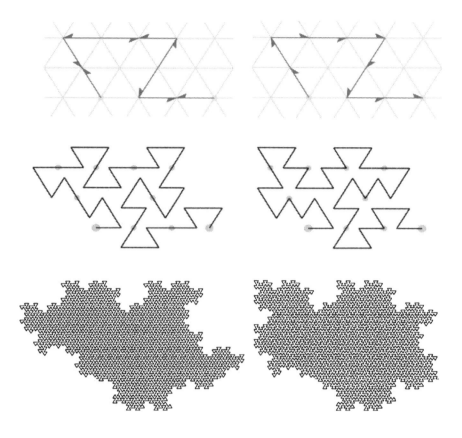

Figure 2.38. Curves of the E(3,0) family: same generator but different transforms

Summary

Now that all five ranks of the taxonomy have been described, let's see how a particular curve—the Dragon of Eve—fits into this hierarchy. In Figure 2.39, the family $G(1,1)^2 = G(0,2)$ has four unique generators that admit plane-filling curves. For sake of illustration, they are rotated by 90 degrees, as if they belonged to the $G(2,0)$ family.

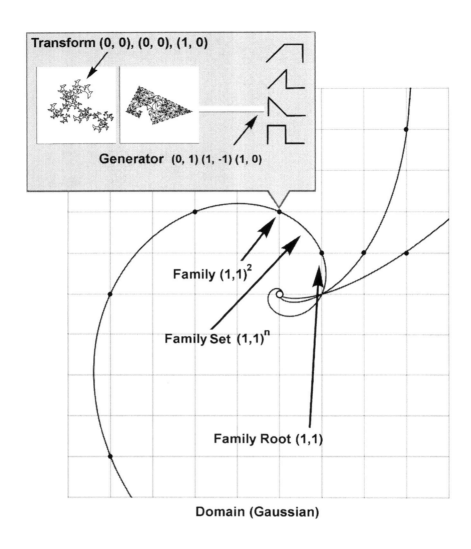

Transform (0, 0), (0, 0), (1, 0)

Generator (0, 1) (1, -1) (1, 0)

Family $(1,1)^2$

Family Set $(1,1)^n$

Family Root (1,1)

Domain (Gaussian)

Figure 2.39. An illustration of how the Dragon of Eve fits in the taxonomic hierarchy

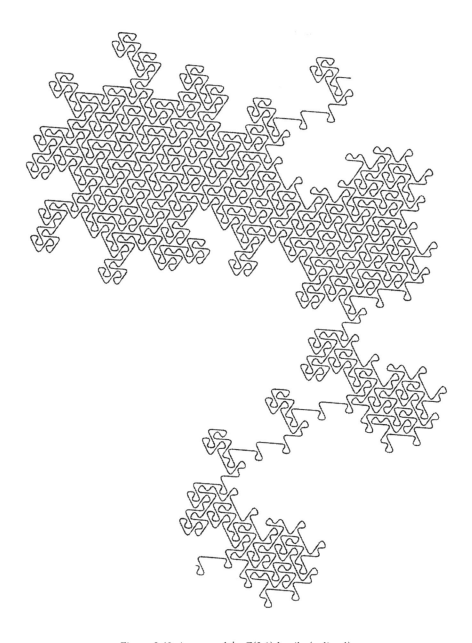

Figure 2.40. A curve of the E(3,1) family (splined)

3

Iteration

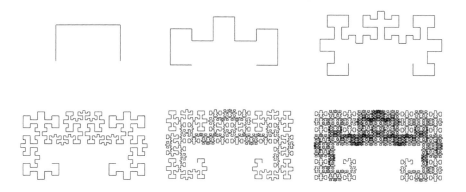

Figure 3.1. A self-avoiding curve of the E(3,0) family

A key thesis in this book is that the complex integers (G and E) can be used as a framework to analyze and classify edge-replacement plane-filling curves. But complex integers can also be used in the process of generating these curves.

As an example, let's explore a technique for creating teragon 2 of the 5-Dragon. It is a member of the G(2,1) family and its norm is 5. It requires no transforms. Figure 3.2. shows the five ordered Gaussian integers of its generator at the top. Teragon 2 can be generated by multiplying five copies of the generator by its own integers, and summing them.

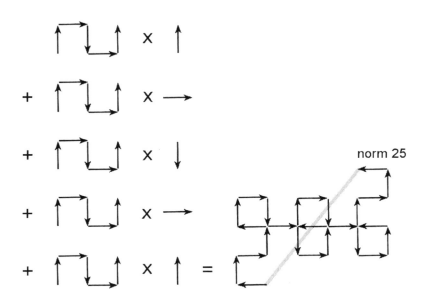

Figure 3.2. Multiplying the 5-dragon generator with itself

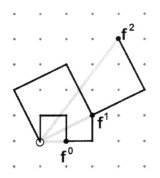

The endpoint of the curve (f) is raised exponentially for each teragon order, as shown in Figure 3.3.

Figure 3.3. Rotation and dilation of 5-Dragon generator

As iteration progresses, the teragons rotate and dilate along the curve of the $G(2,1)^n$ family set, as shown in Figure 3.4.

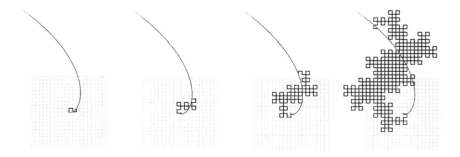

Figure 3.4. As the 5-Dragon iterates, it rotates and dilates along the $G(2,1)^n$ spiral

Figure 3.5 is similar; it shows how teragons of the HH Dragon undergo rotation and dilation, with their endpoints following the power-of-2 spiral with each iteration. Below are three high-order teragons, used to illustrate rotation and dilation.

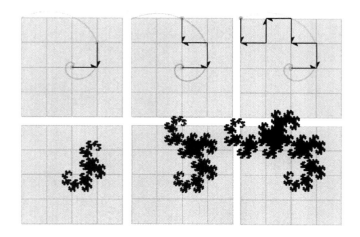

Figure 3.5. Each progressive teragon follows a rotation and a dilation.

Figure 3.6 illustrates a process for generating the first four teragons of a curve from the G(2,2) family, called "Brainfiller" [35].

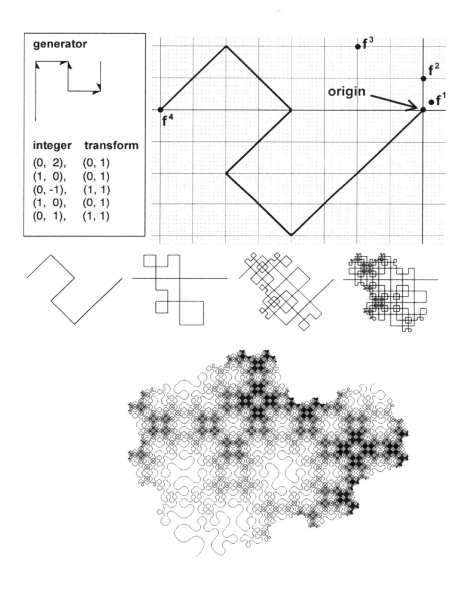

Figure 3.6. Iteration of the Brainfiller curve

The generator for the Brainfiller curve is shown at top-left of Figure 3.6. The family integer G(2,2) has norm 8; it is shown at the far-right as f^1. Raising this integer to the power of 4 (the teragon order) results in the integer G(-64,0), which lies on the power-of-8 spiral. It has norm 4096 and is shown as f^4.

Multiplying the generator by f^3 results in a dilated and rotated copy of the generator, whose endpoint is f^4. With the set of integers lying along the G(2,2) spiral, all possible transforms of the generator can be placed on any segment and the vertices will conform to integer points on the lattice.

A recursive function is used to generate the integers of the curve. Transform state is carried through the recursive steps, determining how the generator is transformed at each step. When recursion is complete, the smallest integer norm in the curve is 1. The teragons of this curve are partially self-contacting. Teragon 5 is shown as a rotated, scaled, and splined rendering at the bottom of the figure.

Transforming back to Family Space

Since this complex number-based technique causes rotation and dilation, computing a teragon of a high order puts the endpoint at a large distance from the origin, with a rotation that may change for each consecutive teragon. The integers can be transformed back to the space of the original generator—to normalize the teragon for purposes of visualization. Essentially, this technique pulls the geometry out of the integer lattice and brings it into the full complex plane, where it can be multiplied arbitrarily.

76

The majority of the examples in this book showing multiple teragons of a single curve have been transformed to occupy the space of the family interval. This transformation allows every curve—regardless of its teragon order (and thus size and rotation)—to be viewed in the family space, as shown with the first six teragons of the 5-Dragon in Figure 3.7.

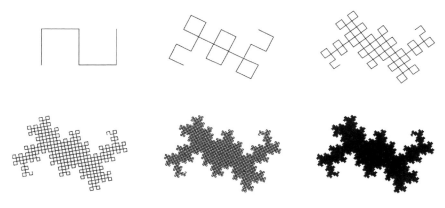

Figure 3.7. Teragons 1-6 of the 5-dragon (scaled to the family integer)

Integer Genetics

Composite integers have a trivial kind of of self-similarity. For instance, the rational integer 35 can be described as 7 *similar* 5's (or 5 *similar* 7's). Highly-composite numbers, such as 60, have more degrees of self-similarity. But only perfect powers have *scaling* self-similarity, making them fractal-like. Consider the rational integer 81, which can be expressed as 3^4. The self-similarity of this perfect power is shown as a stylized partitioning in Figure 3.8.

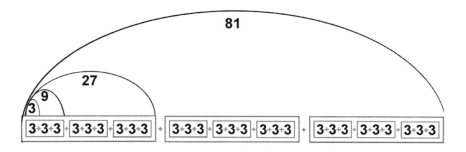

Figure 3.8. Self-similarity of the rational integer 81 as 3^4

The self-similarity of the integer 81 is also expressed in the $E(2,1)^n$ family set (Terdragon teragons 1 through 4) shown in Figure 3.9.

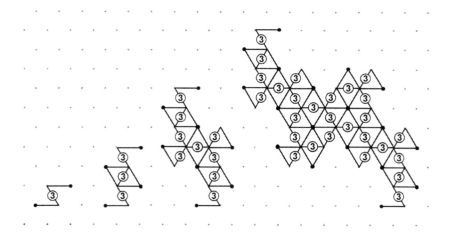

Figure 3.9. Self-similarity of the Eisenstein integers with norms 3, 9, 27, and 81

Integer divisibility and exponentiation are key concepts in this curve-generating technique, and the taxonomy upon which it is based. It is distinct from other kinds of algorithms for computing fractal curves, such as the use of turtle geometry controlled by an L-system.

Turtle geometry uses polar coordinates (angles and lengths). Depending on the curve, the generator's angles and lengths might be real numbers; they may even be irrational—in which case, it is impossible to specify them with full numerical precision. But when the entire specification of the curve is in terms of complex integers (by connecting the points in a lattice), the data footprint becomes relatively small, and computation is more precise, as shown in Figure 3.10.

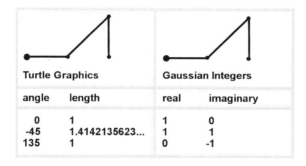

Turtle Graphics		Gaussian Integers	
angle	length	real	imaginary
0	1	1	0
-45	1.4142135623...	1	1
135	1	0	-1

Figure 3.10. Comparing data footprint of turtle geometry vs. integer-based scheme

Reducing the genetic specification of a curve to a small integer representation is an attempt at representing curves using the most fundamental, irreducible distinguishers among them. This technique is an exercise in efficient encoding.

This genetic encoding—when reduced to the smallest possible expression—consists of a single bit to specify the domain (G vs. E), an array of complex integers, and an array of transform pairs (each of which is one bit). With this encoding, the family integer could be left out, since it can be derived from summing the integer array. Figure 3.11 shows an example of this minimal genetic encoding for a curve in the E(2,0) family.

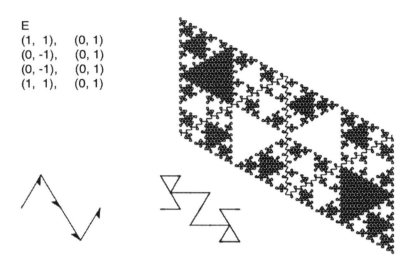

E
(1, 1),   (0, 1)
(0, -1),   (0, 1)
(0, -1),   (0, 1)
(1, 1),   (0, 1)

Figure 3.11. A curve of the E(2,0) family, showing minimal genetic encoding

Figure 3.12 shows Mandelbrot's Snowflake sweep, specified with this abbreviated genetic encoding.

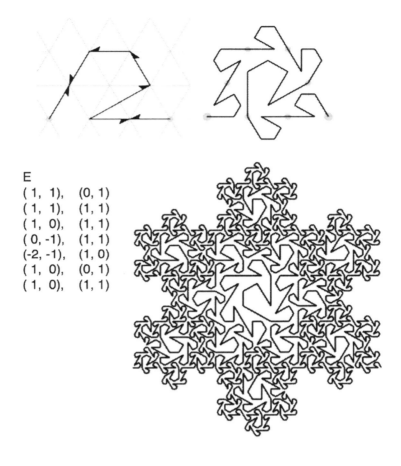

E
(1, 1),   (0, 1)
(1, 1),   (1, 1)
(1, 0),   (1, 1)
(0, -1),   (1, 1)
(-2, -1),   (1, 0)
(1, 0),   (0, 1)
(1, 0),   (1, 1)

Figure 3.12. The Snowflake sweep, showing minimal genetic encoding

Search Space

By reducing the information footprint of the genetic encoding in this way, it becomes easier to search the space of plane-filling curves, because the number of parameters that have to be considered are fewer (and thus, the number of dimensions in the search space).

While searching for curves does require some brute-force computation —especially for larger families, the formulation of this taxonomy has made it much easier to discover the plane-filling curves shown in this book (with more featured in the website fractalcurves.com).

Curves with fractal dimension < 2

Many of the now-familiar edge-replacement curves that were introduced by Mandelbrot can be described using this abbreviated genetic encoding. Not all of them are plane-filling, but since they obey the constraints of the integer lattice, they fit within this taxonomy. Figure 3.13 shows four examples: the Koch curve, the quadradic Koch curve, the Minkowski sausage, and the Monkey's Tree. Since the first three example curves do not require any transforms, these are not included.

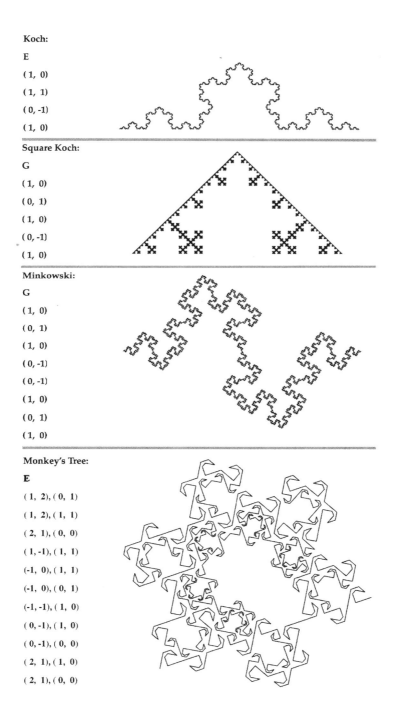

Koch:

E

(1, 0)

(1, 1)

(0, -1)

(1, 0)

Square Koch:

G

(1, 0)

(0, 1)

(1, 0)

(0, -1)

(1, 0)

Minkowski:

G

(1, 0)

(0, 1)

(1, 0)

(0, -1)

(0, -1)

(1, 0)

(0, 1)

(1, 0)

Monkey's Tree:

E

(1, 2), (0, 1)

(1, 2), (1, 1)

(2, 1), (0, 0)

(1, -1), (1, 1)

(-1, 0), (1, 1)

(-1, 0), (0, 1)

(-1, -1), (1, 0)

(0, -1), (1, 0)

(0, -1), (0, 0)

(2, 1), (1, 0)

(2, 1), (0, 0)

Figure 3.13. Genetic encoding of curves with dimension < 2

Figure 3.14. A stylized rendering of a curve with dimension < 2 from the E(3,0) family

4

Morphology

For fractal enthusiasts, the morphological similarities and differences among fractals invites curiosity and wonder. Let's explore the emergent attributes of plane-filling curves, with consideration to how they relate to the concepts covered thus far.

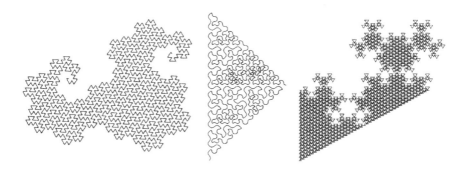

Figure 4.1. Curves from the E(3,1), G(2,2), and E(2,0) families

Mandelbrot suggested that fractals not only stimulate our aesthetic senses; they also serve as models of nature. He used ample illustrations in his introductions of fractals. Mandelbrot was a mathematician working in a discipline that has traditionally been skeptical of visual illustrations, often considering them poor substitutes for (or distractions from) pure mathematical ideas.

This may be true for trained experts with exceptional talents in abstraction…with enough internal processing power to visualize an equation and bring it to life—in the mind's eye. It is also true that a poorly designed illustration can cause ambiguity or distraction. On the other hand, a well-crafted picture is not only worth a thousand words; it also can stimulate the imagination—which motivates understanding, or at least curiosity. With that in mind, let's introduce some visual metaphors from nature.

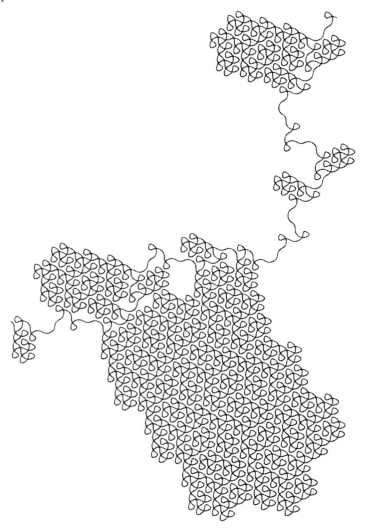

Figure 4.2. A self-crossing curve from the E(3,1) family (splined)

Spine, Flesh, Skin

Like living organisms, fractal curves can only come into existence through a process of iteration. And, like living organisms, the process of growth results in forms that become increasingly complex.

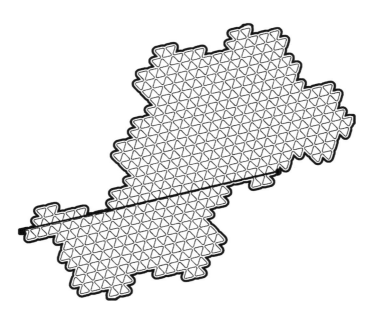

Figure 4.3. Spine, flesh and skin—shown in a curve of the E(3,1) family

Spine

Every family can be represented by a vector that extends from the origin to the family integer. "Spine" is a poetic way of referring to the family integer, visualized as a 2D vector.

All curves of a common family share a common spine, and each family spine is unique. Figure 4.4 shows some examples in both domains.

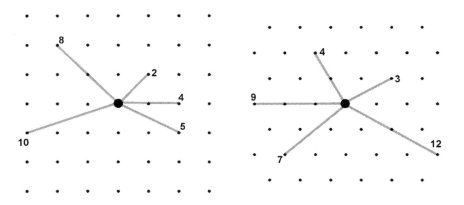

Figure 4.4. Some unique spines, with norms

Spines are not visually interesting, but they are conceptually important. Think of the spine as inherent potential in a family; the *egg*—before cell division starts. It is analogous to the "initiator"—the line segment that serves as the starting point for fractal iteration.

Figure 4.5. Teragons 0-7 of a self-avoiding curve of the E(2,1) family

Flesh

If the spine is the initiator of the curve, then the flesh is the curve itself
—the meandering line that fills a planar area. In a plane-filling fractal
curve, flesh resolves to an infinitely-filled area. The way the curve fills
the area varies greatly among curves. Mandelbrot called this the
"sweep" of the curve [22]. The pattern in this meandering curve can be
seen more clearly in lower-order teragons, where the line is visible, as
shown in Figure 4.6.

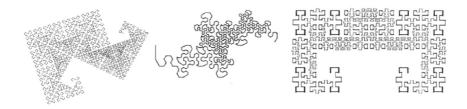

Figure 4.6. Meandering curves constitute the flesh that fills the interior of the body shape

As a plane-filling curve sweeps through its area of the plane, tracing
out its history, it meets itself many times along the way—coming in
close proximity to moments in its past journey. A two-dimensional
polyrhythm is apparent in every curve's sweep—as a distinct pattern
(Figure 4.7).

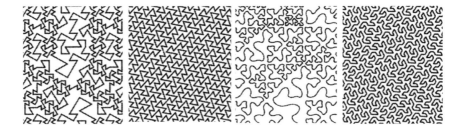

Figure 4.7. Variations in flesh

Power family curves with teragons having multiple-length segments
(such as the Dragon of Eve, Mandelbrot's Snowflake Sweep, and the
curves shown in Figure 4.6) have variable amounts of local structure
distributed within their flesh. This variability extends across more
scales in the higher teragons. Describing the self-similar polyrhythm of
the sweep that forms flesh is not easy, but there are some specific
attributes that are easy to measure—in terms of how a curve can
interact with itself during the sweep. There are four primary categories
of self-interaction in a fractal curve:

1. self-avoiding

2. self-contacting (touching at a lattice point, but not crossing)

3. self-overlapping (sharing a common line segment)

4. self-crossing

These are illustrated in Figure 4.8.

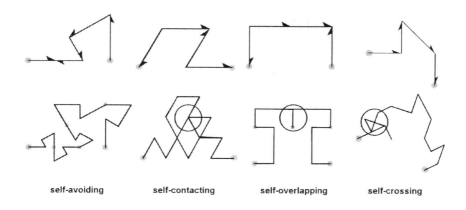

| self-avoiding | self-contacting | self-overlapping | self-crossing |

Figure 4.8. Four ways a curve can interact with itself

Self-Avoiding Curves

Self-avoiding curves have a place of honor in the Kingdom of Curves—being the most clever and acrobatic of them all. A celebrated example is the Gosper curve [37], shown in Figure 4.9 (also called "flowsnake").

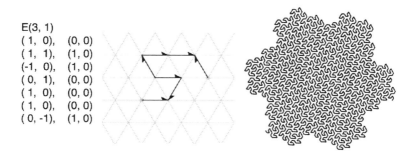

E(3, 1)
(1, 0),   (0, 0)
(1, 1),   (1, 0)
(-1, 0),   (1, 0)
(0, 1),   (0, 0)
(1, 0),   (0, 0)
(1, 0),   (0, 0)
(0, -1),   (1, 0)

Figure 4.9. The Gosper curve

Many variations on the Gosper curve have been discovered by Fukuda, et al. [13], using a clever recursive replacement technique. One of these

91

curves is illustrated in Figure 4.10, with visual overlay. This curve can be described as a member of the E(4,1) family, with norm 13.

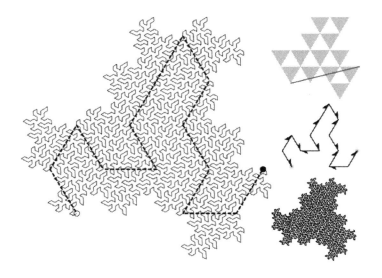

Figure 4.10. a variation of the Gosper curve by Fukuda et al.

Self-avoiding curves often resemble the boundaries between two highly-convoluted domains. More self-avoiding curves will be introduced later in the book.

Self-Contacting Curves

Self-contacting curves touch themselves at points in the lattice, visiting common points in their sweeping histories. They come in many varieties in terms of how they self-contact.

The most regular of these are the "lattice-fillers" or "grid-fillers" (Mandelbrot called these "chunks of lattice"). These curves touch themselves at every lattice point within the body. They can also be called "edge-covering" [2] since they traverse every edge of the grid once, within the body. (Figure 4.11).

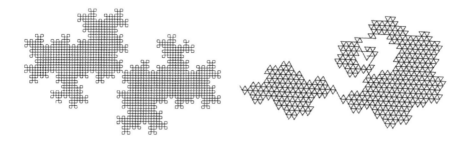

Figure 4.11. The inverted 5-Dragon of the G(5,0) family and a curve of the E(3,1) family

Splined Curves

The angles in a lattice-filling curve can be smoothed-out and *rounded* (splined) to visually separate the contact-points, thus revealing the sweep of the curve. Otherwise it is impossible to see the direction of the sweep. Three examples of classic lattice-filling curves are the HH Dragon, the Terdragon, and the Original Peano curve, shown in Figure 4.12. The curves are splined to reveal their sweeps.

Figure 4.12. Three classic lattice-filling curves (splined)

Another example is shown in Figure 4.13: two different sweeps of the 7-Dragon. Again, the curves are splined to reveal their sweeps. (Since these curves do not require any transforms, they are not included in the genetic description.)

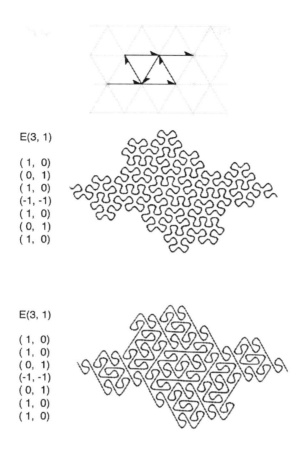

E(3, 1)

(1, 0)
(0, 1)
(1, 0)
(-1, -1)
(1, 0)
(0, 1)
(1, 0)

E(3, 1)

(1, 0)
(1, 0)
(0, 1)
(-1, -1)
(0, 1)
(1, 0)
(1, 0)

Figure 4.13. Two variations (sweeps) of the 7-Dragon (splined)

Unlike lattice-fillers, *partially*-self-contacting curves do not touch themselves at every lattice point within the body. Among the many examples are two subtly-different curves of the G(5,0) family (shown in Figure 4.14, with splined renderings). Their generators each have the same 5 integers of norm 5, but with different transforms. These two curves are related to a tiling described by Bandt et al. [5][6]. At the bottom of the figure are 25 tiles that make up the shape. Like the two 7-

Dragons above, these curves have identical body shapes, but their sweeps are different.

Figure 4.14. Two curves from the G(5,0) family (splined) and a tiling by Bandt

Self-Overlapping Curves

If a generator has overlapping segments, it is guaranteed to produce teragons with overlapping segments. Some generators with no overlapping segments may still produce teragons with overlapping segments, which usually show up after a few iterations. Self-overlapping curves are usually not well-behaved; many of them have tremas and overlapping in their flesh as a result of uneven filling.

But a few well-behaved self-overlapping curves are worth mentioning; they are part of the familiar celebrity set of fractal curve history. These curves include the Peano sweep (partially overlapping) and the G(2,0) version of the Cesàro Sweep (doubly-overlapping everywhere except the bottom edge), shown in Figure 4.15. (The Peano sweep is splined).

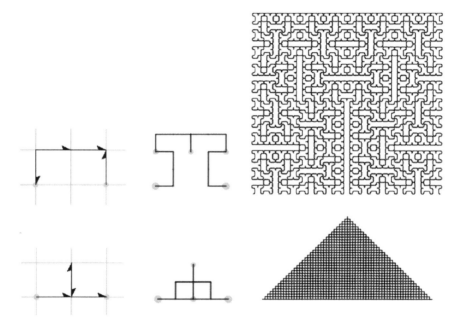

Figure 4.15. Peano sweep and G(2,0) version of the Cesàro sweep are self-overlapping

An interesting self-overlapping curve was identified by Adam Goucher [15], inspired by the pinwheel tiling [27]. Its initiator is a right triangle with sides having lengths 1, 2, and √5 (top of Figure 4.16). It can be represented in the G(5,0) family by way of a reflection, a rotation, and a scaling by √5. The third and fourth integers of the generator are overlapping. At the bottom of figure 4.16 is a splined rendering.

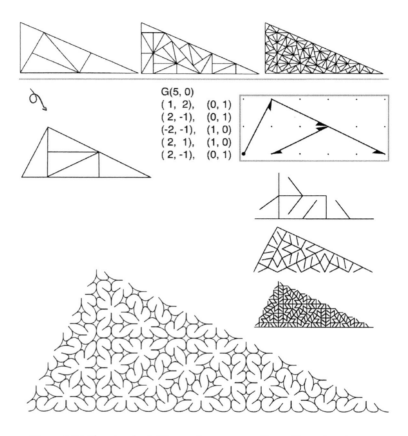

Figure 4.16. The pinwheel tiling and a corresponding self-overlapping curve

Several self-overlapping curves on right triangles have been identified, including one related to a node-replacement curve by Teachout [33] (top of Figure 4.17). Below that is the associated edge-replacement curve, which is splined to reveal its sweep.

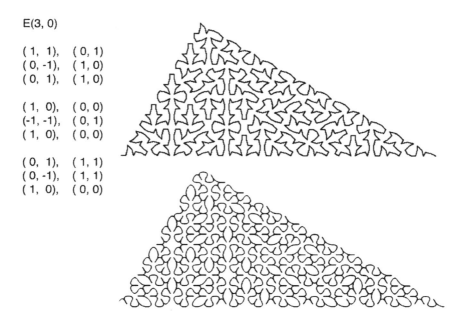

E(3, 0)

(1, 1), (0, 1)
(0, -1), (1, 0)
(0, 1), (1, 0)

(1, 0), (0, 0)
(-1, -1), (0, 1)
(1, 0), (0, 0)

(0, 1), (1, 1)
(0, -1), (1, 1)
(1, 0), (0, 0)

Figure 4.17. A curve by Teachout (top) and a related edge-replacement curve (splined)

Self-Crossing Curves

When considered as an *unordered* collection of line segments that happen to share vertices, self-crossing curves are identical to self-contacting curves. The difference lies in their *sweeps*, where ordering is important. Self-crossing curves can be clever in their Celtic knot-like sweeps. Figure 4.18 shows a self-crossing variation of the 7-Dragon shown at the top of Figure 4.13. In this drawing, the curve is splined so that the tangled rhythm of its sweep can be appreciated.

Figure 4.18. A self-crossing variation of the 7-Dragon (splined)

Skin

Skin is a higher-order emergent attribute of plane-filling curves. It comes into form through the process of iterating teragons—filling ever-finer chunks of the plane with meandering flesh. A boundary is revealed as the process continues, and it becomes crisp to the eye when the teragon order reaches the visual threshold of detail. Other than this visual, impressionistic description, it is difficult to define skin, since it is a chaotic subset of flesh: the bits that lie at the edge of the body shape —which itself is emergent. Perhaps because of this fragmented nature, skins have peculiar properties; most of them are fractal curves in themselves—and they are intimately related to the recursive nature of the flesh within the body shape, through it may not be straightforward to describe this relationship.

Conjecture: the fractal profile of skin is unique to each *family set*. If this is proven to be true, what might the reason be? A single family can have multiple kinds of skin. For example, the E(3,1) family with norm 7 has several curves with "Gosper skin" (having the same jagged profile as the Gosper curve), but also other skins that are completely different, and highly convoluted (Figure 4.19).

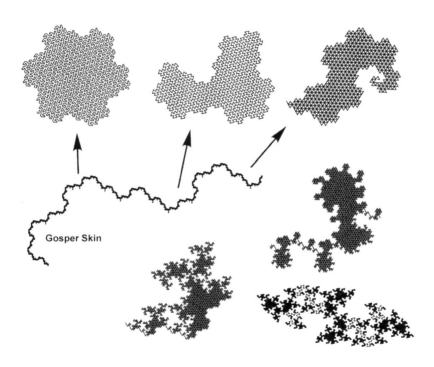

Gosper Skin

Figure 4.19. Gosper skin can be found in several curves of the E(3,1) family

"Skin" denotes the fractal quality of a curve's boundary independent of its gross morphology: the skin's unique signature profile remains intact, no matter what scale of magnification is used to view it. Gross morphology, on the other hand, is a property that holds for one magnification only: the lowest. For example, figure 4.20 shows select sections of the skin of the HH Dragon—described by Chang and Zhang [8].

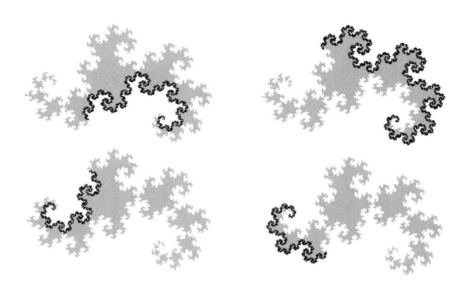

Figure 4.20. HH Dragon skin described by Chang and Zhang

The fractal dimension of skin

The fractal dimension of HH Dragon skin is 1.52362. The fractal dimension of Gosper skin is 1.12915. The skin of the Terdragon (Figure 4.21) has a fractal dimension of 1.26186 (which happens to be the same as the Koch curve).

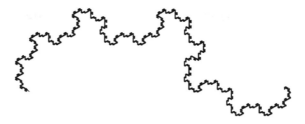

Figure 4.21. Terdragon skin

The fractal dimension of skin varies among curves. Consider the three curves shown in Figure 4.22.

Figure 4.22. Examples of various skins with different fractal dimensions

The curve at left has a skin with dimension 1: any magnification of the boundary appears as a straight edge—with the exception of a set of convex and concave corners, most of which appear near the hook at the top. The skin of the curve in the center of the figure has a high dimension, and at the limit it has an infinity of self-contacting points that pinch-off the body to form an infinity of kissing topological disks. And the curve at right...?

Self-Avoiding Skin vs. Gasket Skin

The curve at the right of Figure 4.22 has a skin whose dimension is ambiguous: the boundary contacts itself so much that it is indistinguishable from its own flesh, creating myriad cavities (tremas). It is similar to a gasket (a fractal with dimension < 2 that has an infinite number of tremas everywhere in its flesh). But can it be called a gasket? It has solidly-filled areas—whose interiors remain solid (locally plane-filling) at arbitrary magnification. Perhaps it could be described as *a plane-filling curve whose skin is a gasket*.

Similar to the way a curve's flesh can interact with itself in many ways, a skin with high dimension may exhibit acrobatic self-contacting yoga. When a curve fills an area that is topologically equal to a disk, then it is a straightforward exercise to identify skin from flesh. It is a self-avoiding skin, making a clear delineation between inside-body and outside-body.

The curve at the right of Figure 4.22 deviates from such topological clarity because its sweep leaves tremas, making it impossible to distinguish its skin from its hole-ridden flesh. Interestingly, a higher-level emergent "boundary" is formed—in this case, it clearly appears straight—forming a broken-triangle-shaped polygon at the macro scale. Rather than try to identify skin from flesh in this class of curve, let's just set it aside as a topological outlier—it is essentially an infinite set of kissing triangles (Figure 4.23).

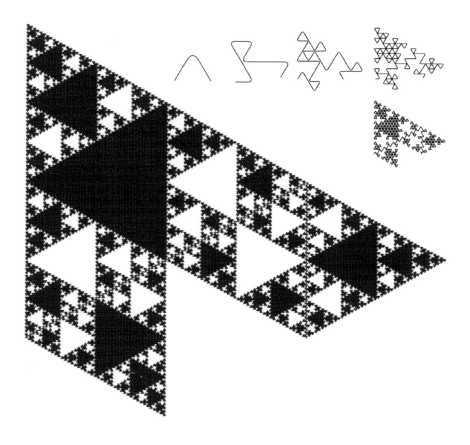

Figure 4.23. A curve of the E(2,0) family

This curve is reminiscent of a fractal described by Mandelbrot [22] (Figure 4.24), as well as the curve shown in Figure 3.11. These gasket-like pseudo-space-filling curves, and some variations of the Sierpinski triangle, share a common feature: "high lacunarity"—a term referring to fractals having *tight clumps* and *large tremas*.

Figure 4.24. A high-lacunarity fractal introduced by Mandelbrot

Area

Fractal generators are often described with the assumption that the distance between the endpoints is 1, as with the initiator Mandelbrot and others have used: the unit interval [0,1]. In contrast, the taxonomy described in this book represents the initiator as a 2D vector equal to the family integer. This is illustrated in Figure 4.25, using the Gosper curve as an example. Unlike Mandelbrot's initiator, the distance between endpoints is $\sqrt{7}$ and each segment has length 1.

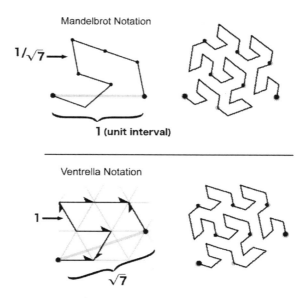

Figure 4.25. Using the family integer as the initiator instead of the unit interval

Family integers have varying norms. Assuming all teragons are normalized to occupy the family space, their areas vary as a function of family norm. This means that curves of higher family norms are larger. The smallest two curves are the HH Dragon and the Pólya curve of the G(1,1) family, each having an area of 1.

Based on experimentation, a few observations have been made in terms of area: if it can be verified that a curve is non-overlapping, then its generator can be used to determine its area. The area of a curve in the Gaussian domain appears to be confined to the range between $f/2$ and f, where f is the family norm. In the Eisenstein domain, the area is confined to the range between $f * \sqrt{3}/2$ and $f * \sqrt{3}$. In the case of self-overlapping curves, the area appears to be smaller, as in the G(2,0) version of the Cesàro sweep, shown in Figure 4.26.

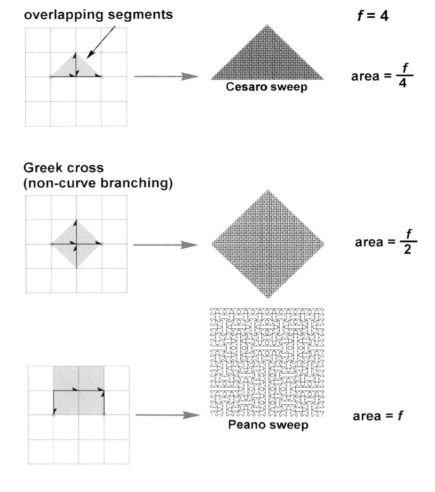

Figure 4.26. Areas of the G(2,0) Cesàro sweep, Greek cross, and Peano sweep

In the Gaussian domain, lattice-filling curves visit every lattice point exactly twice. In the Eisenstein domain, exactly thrice. Self-avoiding curves visit every lattice point *once*, and have the largest areas relative to other curves of the same family. (Conjecture: a plane-filling curve cannot have an area that is larger than its family norm).

Tiling

For curves whose integers all have the same norm (segments of the same length), tiling can be used to visualize the area—using identical tiles (monohedral tiling) that are placed on each line segment of the curve. A few of the basic types of monotiles that can be used are shown in Figure 4.27.

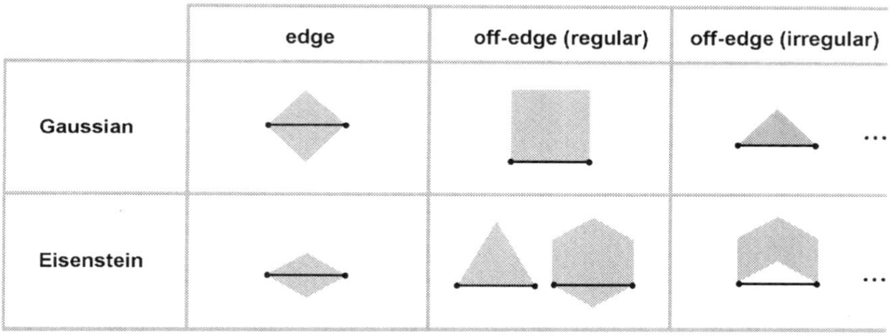

	edge	off-edge (regular)	off-edge (irregular)
Gaussian	◆	▢	▲ ...
Eisenstein	◆	▲ ⬡	⌂ ...

Figure 4.27. Monotiles used for curves with integers having the same norm

Lattice-filling curves can be tiled with edge-tiles, which are symmetric about the line segment, as shown in Figure 4.28.

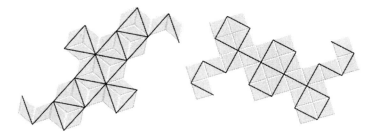

Figure 4.28. Tilings of lattice-filling curves (Terdragon and 5-Dragon)

Self-avoiding curves correspond to off-edge tiles. An example is the use of the regular hexagonal tile for tiling the Gosper curve, shown in Figure 4.29. (The entire shape of the Gosper curve is called the "Gosper Island").

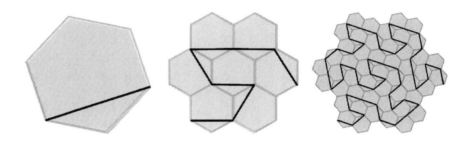

Figure 4.29. Hexagonal tiling in the Gosper curve

In the hexagon at the left of Figure 4.29, the length of the inscribed line segment is $\sqrt{7}$. If this were a segment of unit length, then the area of the hexagon would be $\sqrt{3}/2$. Multiplying that by $\sqrt{7}$ gives ~2.291287: the area of the Gosper curve.

Figure 4.30 shows the four smallest squares in the Gaussian domain whose vertices lie on points in the lattice. Their areas are 1, 2, 4, and 5. The lengths of their edges are $\sqrt{1}$, $\sqrt{2}$, $\sqrt{4}$, and $\sqrt{5}$. Each square (other than the smallest) is accompanied by a plane-filling curve whose family integer traverses a square edge.

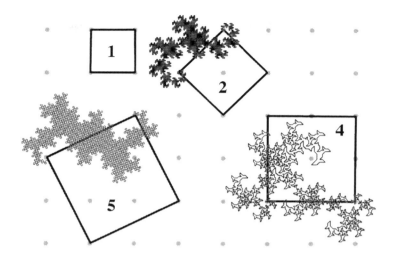

Figure 4.30. Squares in the Gaussian domain with accompanying curves

The HH Dragon (norm 2) and the 5-Dragon (norm 5), which are both lattice-fillers, have areas equal to one-half the area of their associated squares. Because the Dragon of Eve (norm 4) is a self-avoider, the assumption is that its area is equal to that of the square. However, verifying its area is a bit tricky...for the following reason: the Dragon of Eve has integers of varying norms, and so it does not lend itself to regular tiling.

Figure 4.31. shows a progression of square tilings applied to the Dragon of Eve to visualize the area. The sum of the areas of the squares equals the family norm, which is 4. But tremas appear in teragon 3, and in teragon 4, there are tiles that overlap. More gaps and overlaps accumulate with each teragon. So, in this case, monotiling appears to be an unreliable means for determining the area.

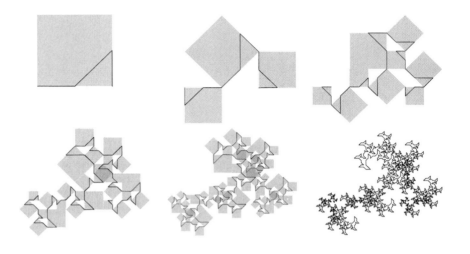

Figure 4.31. Failed attempt at tiling the Dragon of Eve to calculate area

This leaves us with a question:

Is there any way to tile the Dragon of Eve with anything other than small copies of the curve itself? If not, what is the best way to calculate its area?

The "broken hex" monohedral tile shown in Figure 4.27 can be used to tile the "fractal chair," described by Bandt [4]. This is shown in Figure 4.32, accompanied by teragons 0-7 of its associated curve in the E(2,1) family (splined).

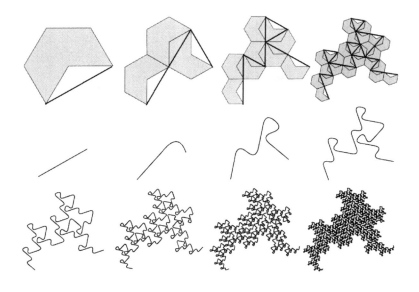

Figure 4.32. The fractal chair and its monohedral tiling, with teragons 0-7 (splined)

Curvature

Curvature refers to the amount of angular *turning* in a curve's path from start to finish. It is defined here as the average angle between consecutive segments in the curve, where "angle" is a real value ranging from 0.0 to 1.0, as illustrated in Figure 4.33.

| 0.0 | 0.25 | 0.5 | 0.75 | 1.0 |

Figure 4.33. Values for curvature between connected segments in a curve

In the context of a single family, a larger area appears to be correlated with lower curvature. Consider the generators of two curves of the G(2,2) family, shown in Figure 4.34. The top curve is a lattice-filler, and the bottom curve is a self-avoider. Both curves have the same spine of length √8, shown at left.

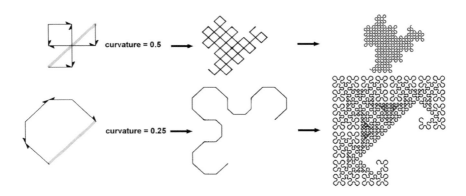

Figure 4.34. Differences in curvature in the G(2,2) family

Curvature is higher in lattice-fillers (as high as $1/2$ in the Gaussian domain [e.g., 5-Dragon], and as high as $2/3$ in the Eisenstein domain [e.g., Terdragon]). It appears to be lower in self-avoiding curves. Curves with higher curvature are able to pack more *stuff* into a smaller *space*, and thus have smaller areas. However, this is not true in all cases; for example, the two 7-Dragons shown in Figure 4.13 have the same area but different curvatures. In this case, the difference shows up only in the nature of the curve's sweep—not its area.

McKenna observed that plane-filling curves inscribed in equilateral triangles are *always* self-contacting and never self-avoiding. Conversely, there exist self-avoiding curves with square body shapes [23]. This is related to the observation that it requires more curvature to pack a curve into an equilateral triangle than it does to pack a curve of the same length into a square, assuming both shapes have the same edge length.

Point-Symmetrical Curves

Many curves have point-symmetry: their shapes remain identical when rotated 180 degrees. This symmetry is apparent in the generator as well as in the associated teragons. Point-symmetric curves appear to be the result of the ordering of the integers in the generator having a *palindrome* form—being identical when read backwards. There are no 180-rotation transforms in the generators of these curves, since the generators themselves have point symmetry, thus 180-rotating has no effect. Figure 4.35. shows a few such curves. There are no point-symmetrical curves in the G(1,1) family or the G(2,0) family. Are there any other families *without* point-symmetry? If not, why?

Figure 4.35. A few examples of curves with point-symmetry

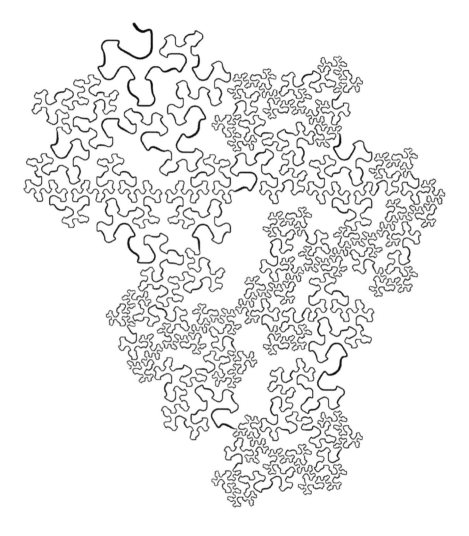

Figure 4.36. A stylized curve of the E(3,0) family with dimension < 2

5

Family Resemblances

Fractal curves exhibit *data amplification* upon iteration of their relatively simple genetic origins. There is wonderful diversity among the plane-filling curves. And there are also obvious similarities. These curves—being constrained by the integer lattice—have certain properties that can be described algebraically. Many of the resemblances among curves are determined by where they lie within their family hierarchies—and some of these resemblances can be characterized using integer math.

Primes, Composites, Roots, and Powers

Prime numbers are fundamental in multiplication. They are the primitive building blocks of divisibility. Curves of prime root families are likewise fundamental. For instance, prime curves can only have integers that are units.

The product of any two integers with norms > 1 is a composite integer. Composite root families have curves that are identical to the curves of their associated divisor families (except they are larger, and possibly rotated). Consider the rational integer 10: 2 and 5 are its divisors. Similarly, all of the curves in the $G(1,1)$ family and all of the curves in the $G(2,1)$ family can be found in the $G(3,1)$ family, which is a *composite root family*. Figure 5.1 shows three curves of the $G(3,1)$ family with norm 5. The two at the bottom are identical to curves found in the $G(1,1)$ and $G(2,1)$ families, except they are larger and rotated. The curve shown at the top is unique only to the G(3,1) family (and its descendants/multiples).

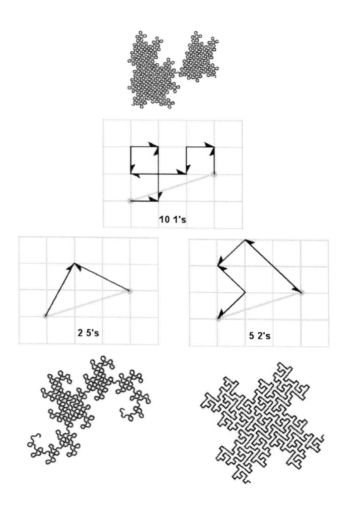

Figure 5.1. The G(3,1) family has curves identical to those of the G(1,1) and G(2,1) families

You could say the composite root families have a *larger phenotype space* than prime root families, since they possess curves that are isometric to the root curves of their constituent divisor families.

Flesh-Creative Power Descendants

When it comes to family resemblances in curves, exponentiation is more exciting than multiplication. The phenotype space is larger among power families. As you journey along a family set, self-similarity grows, not just in terms of the scaled-up repetition of divisor curves, but in the creative hybridizing of their ancestry. For instance, Figure 5.2 shows the beginning of the $G(1,1)^n$ family set. The HH dragon is shown at the root, with progressively more complex variations in the $G(1,1)^2$ and $G(1,1)^3$ families.

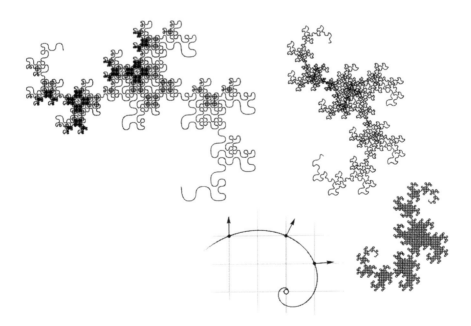

Figure 5.2. The first three curves of the $G(1,1)^n$ family set descended from the HH Dragon

There are apparently many more flesh-variations of the HH Dragon body shape along this family set. Figure 5.3 shows the HH dragon and six of its descendants. They are all splined and normalized to the space of the HH Dragon.

Figure 5.3. The HH Dragon with five descendants in the $G(1,1)^n$ family set

The variety of a family grows with exponentiation (relative to its order in the family set). In power families, many body shapes are isometric to those of their ancestors (in families closer to the start of the family set), but their flesh can be more complex, owing to the fact that they can have multiple-length segments. Figure 5.4 shows three curves of the E(2,1) family (left side) associated with more complex-flesh curves in the E(2,1)² family (right side) that have the same body shape. Rotations and scales have been normalized to emphasize only differences in flesh.

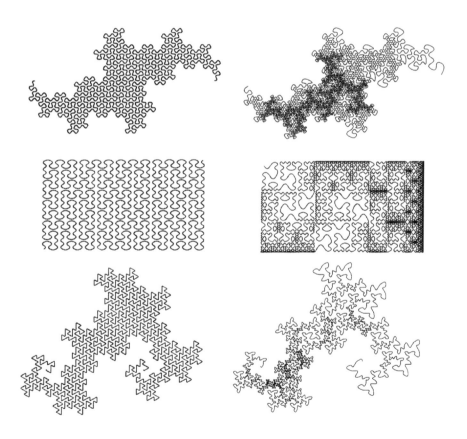

Figure 5.4. Some curves in the E(2,1) family (left), shown with descendants (right)

Another example of morphological similarity within a family set is shown in Figure 5.5. The first four teragons of the Dragon of Eve are shown in the left column. The other two columns show the first four teragons of related curves from the $G(1,1)^2$ and $G(1,1)^3$ families. They are normalized to the family space of the Dragon of Eve for comparison. Tergaon 4 of the curve from the $G(1,1)^3$ family is shown larger at bottom-right (splined). Notice how the "horn" of the Dragon of Eve teragon has an extra protrusion added to make the other teragons. This has an effect not unlike iterating the teragon to the next order, but only doing it on the middle segment. Each of these curves are self-avoiding. Is it possible that similar protrusions could be added to the horns of consecutive relatives, resulting in more curly Dragons?

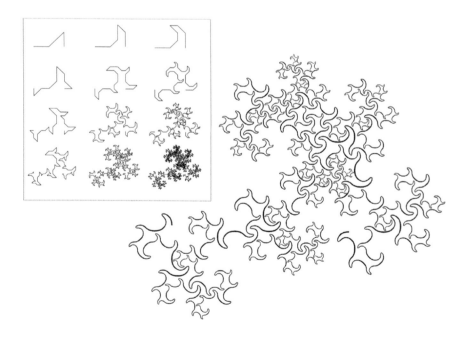

Figure 5.5. Top: Dragon of Eve and relatives in the $G(1,1)^2$ set; bottom: third relative

A similar technique can be applied to Mandelbrot's Quartet by representing it in the G(5,0) family with each integer having norm 5. One of its segments is replaced with a copy of the original generator, to create a more elaborate sweep (Figure 5.6).

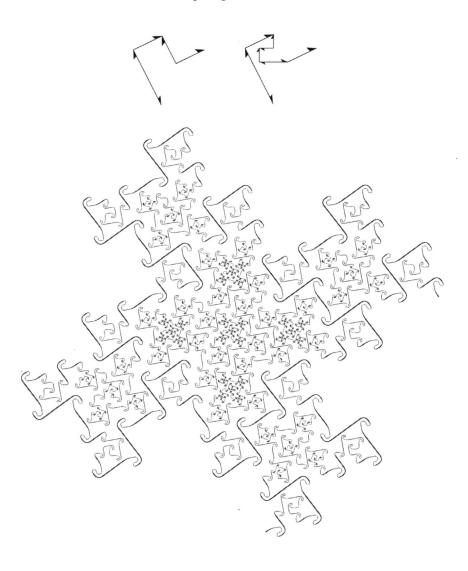

Figure 5.6. Modified version of Mandelbrot's Quartet, with stylized rendering

Axis-aligned curves

A subset of the complex integers (of both domains) is the set of rational integers. They lie on the real axis. Figure 5.7 shows the beginning of the positive side of this set in the Gaussian domain. The diagonal axis has norms that are twice those of the real axis.

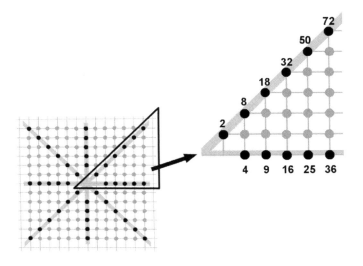

Figure 5.7. Axis-aligned norms in the Gaussian domain

Let's refer to the orthogonal axes in Figure 5.7 as "primary axes," and the diagonal axes as "secondary axes." Each axis starts at the origin and extends out to infinity. The Gaussian domain has four primary (orthogonal) axes and four secondary (diagonal) axes. The Eisenstein domain has six primary axes and six secondary axes. Primary axes correspond to the directions of the units.

Here's an observation: the families that lie on these axes appear to be the only ones that include curves with straight-edge skins (skins with a fractal dimension of 1). For example, curves with square or equilateral triangle body shapes can only be found along the primary axes. Two such curves are shown in Figure 5.8 (splined).

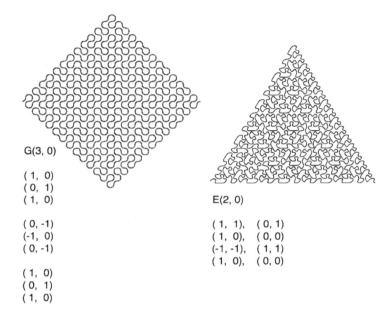

G(3, 0)	
(1, 0)	
(0, 1)	
(1, 0)	E(2, 0)
(0, -1)	(1, 1), (0, 1)
(-1, 0)	(1, 0), (0, 0)
(0, -1)	(-1, -1), (1, 1)
	(1, 0), (0, 0)
(1, 0)	
(0, 1)	
(1, 0)	

Figure 5.8. Two (splined) curves with regular polygon boundaries

The famous Sierpinski arrowhead curve is a gasket of the E(2,0) family, which lies on the primary axis. Like the example at the right in Figure 5.8, it occupies a regular triangle—*but only partially,* because its fractal dimension is only 1.5849 (Figure 5.9).

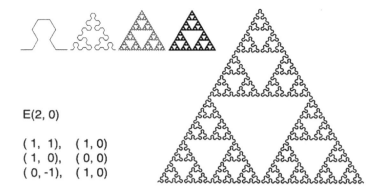

E(2, 0)

(1, 1),   (1, 0)
(1, 0),   (0, 0)
(0, -1),   (1, 0)

Figure 5.9. The Sierpinski arrowhead curve

Question: is the Sierpinski arrowhead curve self-avoiding? It would seem so, from looking at the first few teragons. However, at infinity, it is identical to the Sierpinski Gasket, which is an infinite number of infinitely small kissing triangles (Figure 5.10).

Figure 5.10. The Sierpinski Gasket

By the way: in the same family as the Sierpinski arrowhead curve (E(2,0)) is a curious relative, affectionately called "Sierpinski Family". It has its own way of expressing self-similarity (Figure 5.11).

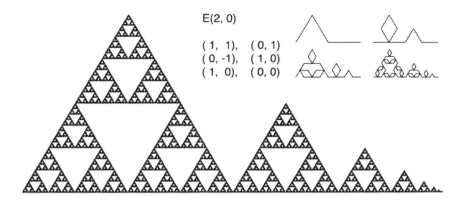

Figure 5.11. The Sierpinski Family

Dieter Steemann identified a variation of the Sierpinski Family that is self-avoiding [32], using an L-System (Figure 5.12). Might there be a way to describe his generator in the context of this taxonomy?

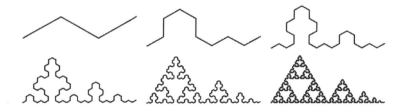

Figure 5.12. Steemann's variation of the Sierpinski Family

Curves with straight-edge skins can also be found in families lying on the secondary axes (although regular polygon body shapes can only be found in families lying on the primary axis). Two such curves are shown in Figure 5.13.

127

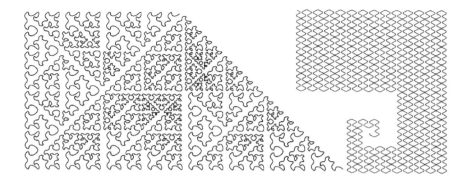

Figure 5.13. Two curves from secondary axis families with straight skins (splined)

Curves that lie on an axis can have transformations that include reflections, due to the bilateral symmetry about the axis.

Families that do not lie on an axis have no straight-skinned curves (at least none have been found in the formulation of this taxonomy). The reason may have to do with the fact that there is no way to trace a straight path from the origin to the family integer that visits any lattice points along the way. Their skins require diversions from the axis of the spine. As an example, Figure 5.14 shows the six plane-filling curves of the G(2,1) family, with norm 5.

Figure 5.14. Curves of the G(2,1) family

This set includes the 5-Dragon and Mandelbrot's Quartet. Similar skins can be detected in four of the curves. None of the skins are straight.

Recall how the 5-Dragon generator cannot be reflected about its family integer because this would cause it to break out of the lattice. Now, let's see what happens if we transform the 5-Dragon generator so that it corresponds to two families of norm 25. The generators shown at the left of Figure 5.15 are each made up of five integers of norm 5. This illustrates how two rotations of this generator can be associated with two different integers having norm 25.

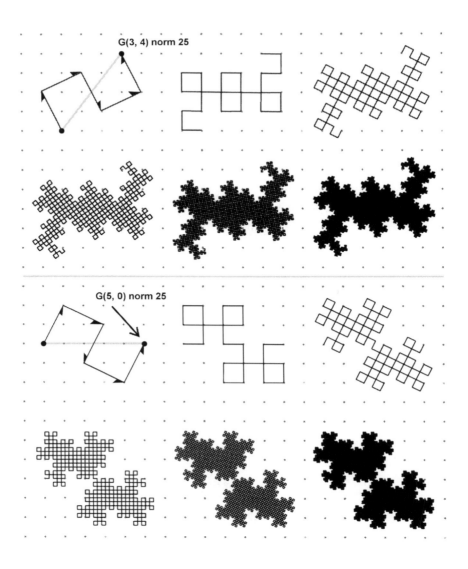

Figure 5.15. 5-Dragon and inverted 5 Dragon shown in two families with norm 25

The integer G(3,4) shown at top is a perfect power whose root is G(2,1). The integer shown at bottom: G(5,0) is the product of G(2,1) and its conjugate G(2,-1). (The conjugate of a complex number is equal to the number with its imaginary component negated.) Multiplying a complex number by its conjugate always results in the product lying on the positive real axis. As a result, the segments in this generator can be reflected. Reflecting all of them results in a jagged butterfly shape, called "Inverted 5-Dragon". Curiously, it appears that this generator *allows only reflected segments.*

There are undoubtedly more such discoveries to be made, and considerations to be explored…perhaps relating to the fact that G(5,0) is not a perfect power, yet it is the product of conjugates (both having the same norm). With such discoveries beyond the current horizon, this taxonomy may need to be modified or enhanced.

Twin Twins

Not all curves that are members of axis-aligned families have straight skins. Let's take a brief diversion and visit the Twindragon; a fractal shape with point-symmetry. It can be created by conjoining a HH dragon with a 180-rotated copy (Figure 5.16).

Figure 5.16. Twindragon as a pertiling of two HH dragons

131

Figure 5.17 shows three curves of the G(2,2) family with fractal skin. The first two are similar to the Twindragon. But unlike the Twindragon, the body shapes of these curves are comprised of different-sized "broken" Twindragons—kissing at fractally-distributed pinch-points. What accounts for these curious body shapes?

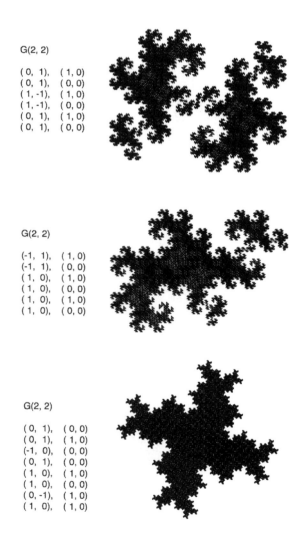

G(2, 2)

(0, 1),   (1, 0)
(0, 1),   (0, 0)
(1, -1),   (1, 0)
(1, -1),   (0, 0)
(0, 1),   (1, 0)
(0, 1),   (0, 0)

G(2, 2)

(-1, 1),   (1, 0)
(-1, 1),   (0, 0)
(1, 0),   (1, 0)
(1, 0),   (0, 0)
(1, 0),   (1, 0)
(1, 0),   (0, 0)

G(2, 2)

(0, 1),   (0, 0)
(0, 1),   (1, 0)
(-1, 0),   (0, 0)
(0, 1),   (0, 0)
(1, 0),   (1, 0)
(1, 0),   (0, 0)
(0, -1),   (1, 0)
(1, 0),   (1, 0)

Figure 5.17. Three curves of the G(2,2) family

McKenna's Curves

Douglas McKenna developed categories for families of plane-filling curves based on square and triangular grids [23]. Some of them are described here in the context of this taxonomy. Figure 5.18 shows the "E-curve" at top (generator and 2nd teragon). In this context, the E-curve can be described as a member of the G(5, 0) family, having norm 25. It is an axis-aligned, self-avoiding curve with a square body. The E-curve is the first in a series of self-avoiding curves that follow a certain logic for generator growth, shown at bottom. These are called "SquaRecurves". The "order" of the generator is equal to the square root of the family norm (the Euclidean distance between generator's endpoints, which lie on the real axis). Only odd-numbered orders admit curves in this series.

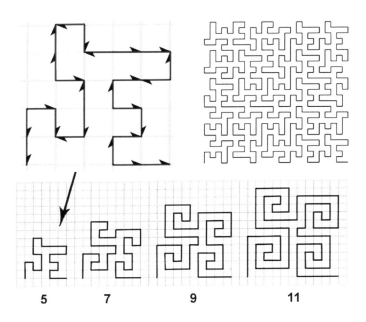

Figure 5.18. The E curve (top) and the first few SquaRecurve generators.

133

Two other series of self-avoiding curves described by McKenna are shown in Figure 5.19. These include "Frenzies" (left) and "Eddies" (right). In this figure, the generators have been rotated and scaled to show how they fit within the family structure of this taxonomy. Notice that curve (a) is Mandelbrot's Quartet, and that curve (b) is the G(3,2) self-avoider we saw earlier in Figure 2.18.

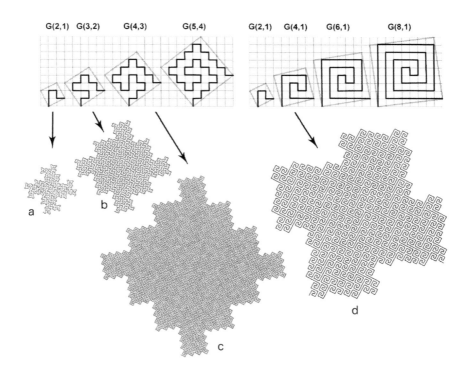

Figure 5.19. Frenzies and Eddies

Relation to Node-Replacement Curves

Here's a conjecture: every edge-replacement curve that permits monohedral tiling (i.e., all norms are identical) has an associated self-avoiding node-replacement curve, and the nodes correspond to the centers of the curve's tiles. Below are some of these correlations.

Peano/Hilbert

The Hilbert curve was shown earlier as an example of a node-replacement curve. Figure 5.20 demonstrates how the Hilbert curve and the Peano sweep both undergo the same transform logic, as illustrated by the orientations of the tiles numbered 1 through 4.

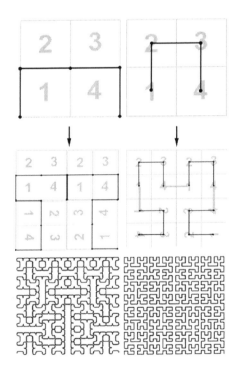

Figure 5.20. Peano sweep (splined) compared to the Hilbert curve

The tiling of the Peano sweep has the same *scanning order* as the nodes of the Hilbert curve. This comparison was also made by McKenna [23] and others.

These transforms bring to mind the behaviors of turbulent fluids. Imagine an upward surge of fluid, as illustrated in Figure 5.21. As the dark fluid surges upward, the light-colored fluid around it gets pulled inward, creating a "neck", as shown at top-right, and the dark fluid bifurcates at the top. A similar shape can be seen in the second teragons for the Peano sweep and the Hilbert curve.

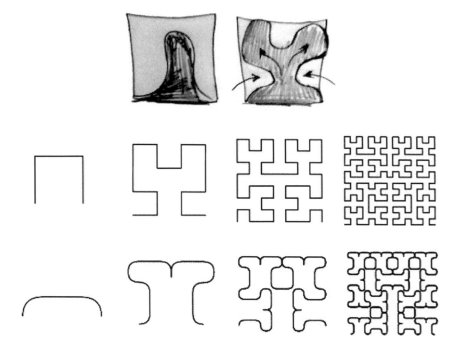

Figure 5.21. fluid-like forms in the Hilbert curve and Peano sweep (splined)

Eisenstein Variation of Peano/Hilbert

The Peano sweep is a partially-self-avoiding curve, with an off-edge square tiling. There is an analogous curve in the Eisenstein domain: a triangular sweep with an off-edge triangle tiling. And, like the Peano sweep, this curve has a node-replacement counterpart, shown in Figure 5.22.

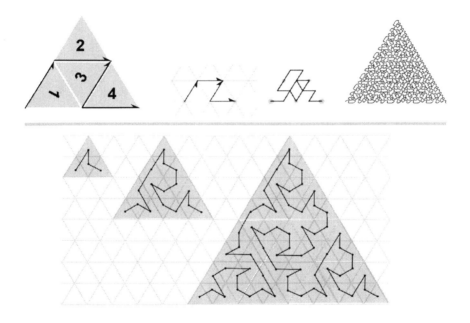

Figure 5.22. A triangle sweep of the E(2,0) family, and a node-replacement counterpart.

Similar curves have been explored by Teachout [33], and Fiedorowicz [12].

Node-Gosper

Figure 5.23 shows a node-replacement version of the Gosper curve. The numerical order is plotted in the middle of each tile of the Gosper curve. These points are connected to form the node Gosper generator.

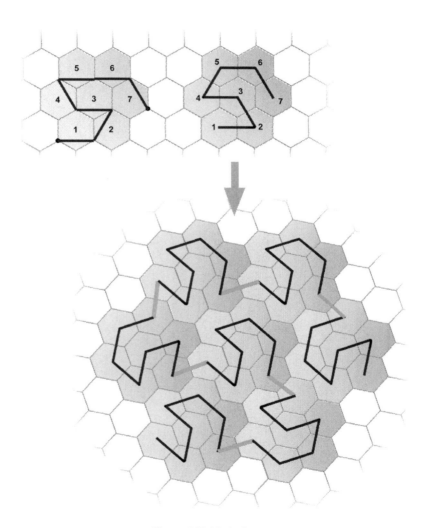

Figure 5.23. Node Gosper

138

Node-Quartet

Figure 5.24 shows a node-replacement version of Mandelbrot's Quartet.

Figure 5.24. The Node Quartet

Node-Pinwheel

The curve that corresponds to the pinwheel tiling described earlier has a node-replacement version, also suggested by Goucher [15].

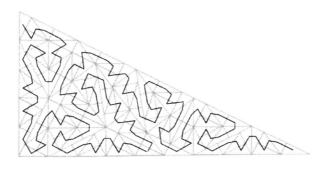

Figure 5.25. Node-replacement curve on Pinwheel tiling

Sierpinski/Cesàro

The Sierpinski curve can be described as a node-replacement version of
the Cesàro sweep. Figure 5.26 shows two variations of the Cesàro
sweep. At the top of the figure is the version described by Mandelbrot,
which is rotated here because it is treated as a member of the G(1,1)
family. At the bottom is the G(1,1)^2 version. In both versions, an off-
edge right triangle is used to tile the area. The mid-points of the tiles
are connected to create the Sierpinski curve. Notice how the 180-rotated
segments in the G(1,1) version cause alternating teragon profiles, which
do not appear in the G(1,1)^2 version.

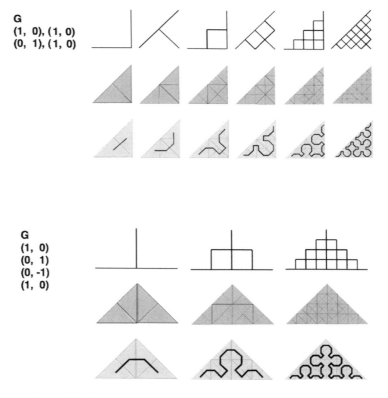

Figure 5.26. Relationship between Cesàro sweep and Serpinski curve

140

Node-Peano

Two variations of the Peano curve provide another example of the relationship between node-replacement and edge-replacement (Figure 5.27). Both of their generators occupy a 3x3 grid, and they map to each other by way of a 45-degree rotation (bottom row).

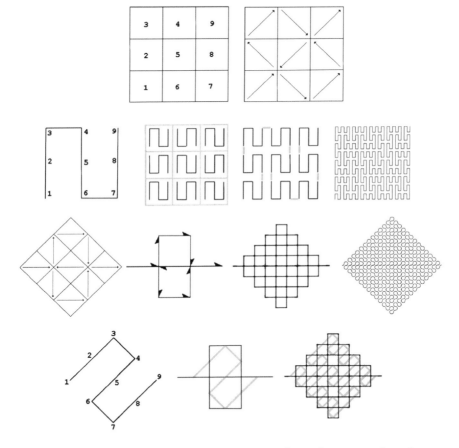

Figure 5.27. Peano curve: tiling, node-replacement, edge-replacement, and overlap

Alexander Bogomolny identified a set of variations of the Peano curve by applying reflections to the tiles of the generator [7]. These reflections would have no visual effect in the edge-replacement version, since the generator is symmetrical about the segment. But they are easily seen in the node-replacement version. Bogomolny identified a total of 272 variations, given all combinations of reflections. A teragon of one such variation is shown in Figure 5.28.

Figure 5.28. One of 272 variations of the node-replacement Peano curve, using reflections

Within the same family (G(3,0)), a variation of the Wunderlich curve called the "Peano-Meander curve" (a node-replacement curve) has a complementary edge-replacement curve of the G(3,0) family (bottom of Figure 5.29). The ordering of its nine tiles allows nine continuous segments to be drawn, starting at G(0, 0,) and ending at G(3, 0), such that each segment coincides with a unique tile edge. Similar to the Peano sweep, this curve's generator has overlapping segments (5th and 6th).

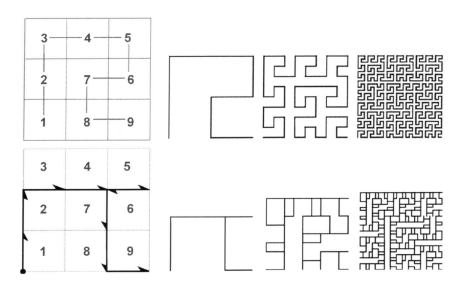

Figure 5.29. A Wunderlich curve and its associated edge-replacement curve

As proposed before, if a monohedral tiling can be associated with an edge-replacement curve, then it is possible to create a complimentary node-replacement curve by connecting the midpoints of the tiles. But it seems the reverse is not always true. Some node-replacement curves (e.g., the Moore curve [24] and the Z-order (Lebesgue) curve—Figure 5.30) do not have associated edge-replacement curves, because of the spatial ordering of their tiles. In the Moore curve (top), which consists of 4 scaled-down, rotated versions of the Hilbert curve, the first and last tiles are *adjacent*. In the Z-order curve (bottom), there are consecutive nodes that jump between *non-adjacent* tiles.

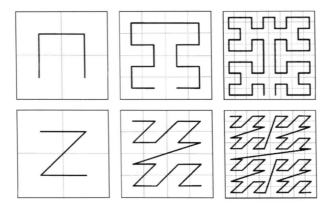

Figure 5.30. The Moore and Z-order curves have no associated edge-replacement curves

144

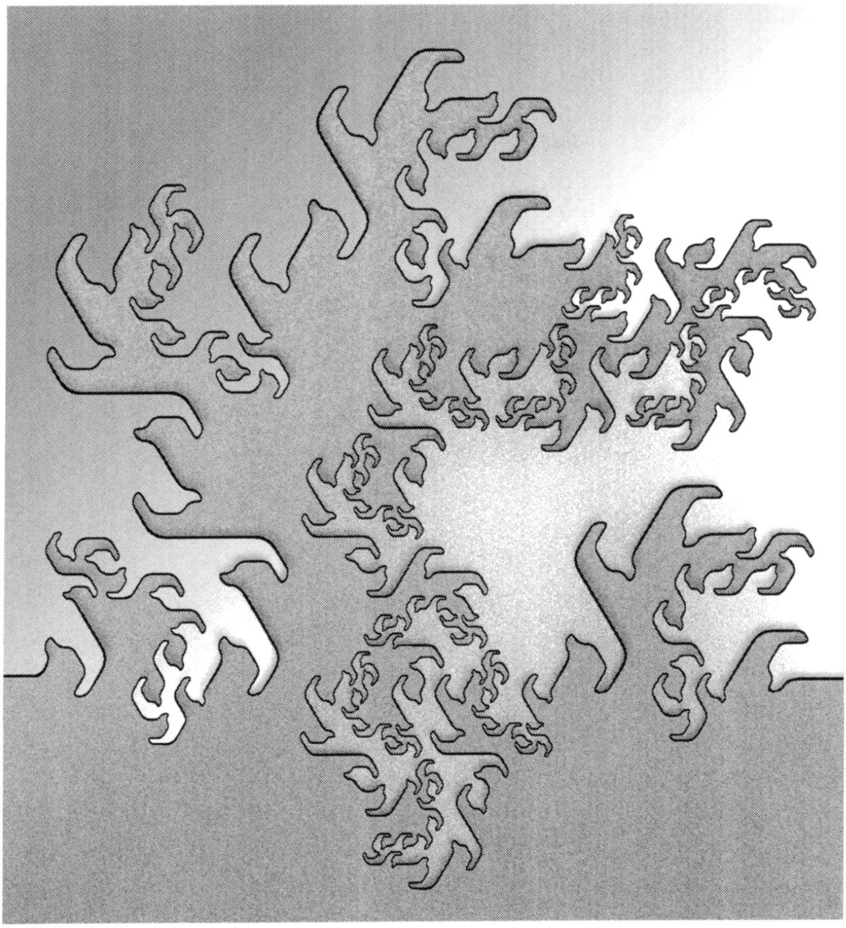

Figure 5.31. Stylized curve with dimension < 2 that partially fills the Koch snowflake

6

Undiscovered Curiosities

The invention of the telescope allowed astronomers to peer deeper into the cosmos. The invention of the microscope allowed biologists to peer deeper into the inner workings of cells. Although true fractals are *Platonic* entities—occupying an abstract mathematical realm—it is hard to avoid the feeling that these mathematical objects lay hidden, like stars and cells, unavailable to the human eye until the right tools come along to bring them out of darkness.

Here is a question: are fractals designed by humans or discovered by humans? Let us not rush to a binary answer, and instead savor the question. Amazing fractal patterns do appear in nature, untouched by the human hand. The information dynamic resulting from running a recursive function on a computer has similarities to many dynamical systems in nature. Thus, the computer can be considered as a tool to visualize aspects of nature.

Software and graphics technology have helped inspire new mathematical tools and ideas that made it possible to discover the fractal gems that we can now calculate at lightning speeds. This power of calculation never could have been imagined when Giuseppi Peano drew his nine-segment curve in 1890.

Conclusion

One goal of the taxonomy and associated techniques covered in this book is to provide a framework for describing several familiar plane-filling curves…under one system. It also provides a methodology for discovering more curves, including the infinity of beasts that lie far from home—far from their origins in the Gaussian and Eisenstein domains. Imagine exploring the far reaches of a family set—rich with genealogical self-similarity; we will find amazing new curves with complex variations on their ancestry.

The reason a taxonomy is possible may have something to do with the iterative nature of genesis, and the presence of certain constraints that encourage structures to emerge. Like biological organisms, these constraints come into play when genotypes guide the expression of phenotypes through recursion. For these curves, the lattice of complex integers corresponds to some of those constraints. This book lays the foundations of a framework for categorizing self-similar, plane-filling fractal curves. Mathematicians, geometers, designers, and anyone with a playful curious mind, will hopefully find it useful as a context for more discoveries—to reveal more amazing and beautiful fractal curves.

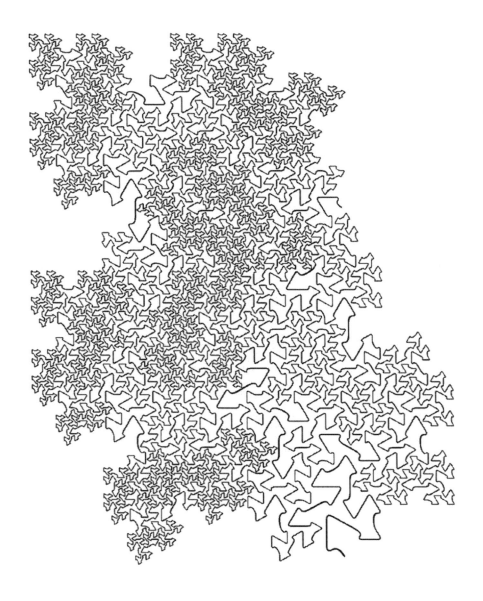

Figure 6.1. A self-avoiding curve of the E(2,1)² family

References

[1] Abelson, H., and diSessa, A. *Turtle Geometry*. MIT Press, 1986.

[2] Arndt. J. Plane-filling Curves On All Uniform Grids. http://
informatique.umons.ac.be/algo/csd8/slides/Arndt_CSD8_long.pdf
(https://arxiv.org/pdf/1607.02433.pdf)

[3] Bader, Michael. *Space-Filling Curves - An Introduction with Applications in Scientific Computing*. Springer Science and Business Media, 2012.

[4] Bandt, C. Self-similar tilings and patterns described by mappings. Mathematics of Aperiodic Order (ed. R. Moody) Proc. NATO Advanced Study Institute C489, Kluwer 1997, 45-83.

[5] Bandt, C. Mekhontsev, D. and Tetenov, A. A single fractal pinwheel tile. Proc. Amer. Math. Soc. 146, 1271–1285 (2018).

[6] Bandt, C. Personal communication, 2017.

[7] Bogomolny, A. Plane Filling Curves: All Peano Curves. https://www.cut-the-knot.org/Curriculum/Geometry/PeanoComplete.shtml

[8] Chang, A. and Zhang, T. On the Fractal Structure the Boundary of Dragon Curve: http://www.coiraweb.com/poignance/math/Fractals/Dragon/Bound.html

[9] Davis, C. and Knuth, D. Number Representations and Dragon Curves. Journal of Recreational Mathematics. 3 (1970), 66-81, 133-149

[10] Dekking, Michel. Paperfolding Morphisms, Planefilling Curves, and Fractal Tiles. *Theoretical Computer Science*, 414, (2012) 20-37

[11] Fathauer, R. Fractal art, published on https://www.mathartfun.com/robertfathauer.com/index.html

[12] Fiedorowicz, Z. . √4 triangle grid family triangle curve variation, published at: http://www.math.osu.edu/~fiedorow/math655/examples2.html

[13] Fukuda, M. Shimizu and G. Nakamura, New Gosper Space Filling Curves, Proceedings of the International Conference on Computer Graphics and Imaging (CGIM2001) 34--38 . 2001

[14] Gilbert. W. Fractal Geometry Derived from Complex Bases. The Mathematical Intelligencer. vol. 4. 1982

[15] Goucher. A. (personal communication) Blog post: Complex Projective 4-Space blog: https://cp4space.wordpress.com/

[16] Haverkort, H. Three pretty plane-filling curves, December, 2016. available online at: http://herman.haverkort.net/lib/exe/fetch.php?media=research:pretty-curves.pdf

[17] Hilbert, D. "Über die stetige Abbildung einer Linie auf ein Flächenstück", Math. Ann., 1891 (38), pp. 459-460.

[18] Hutchinson, John, E. Fractals and Self-Similarity. Indiana University Mathematics Journal. Vol. 30, No. 5 (September–October, 1981), pp. 713-747

[19] Irving, G. and Segerman, H. Developing Fractal Curves. Journal of Mathematic in the Arts. Vol 6, 2013, Issue 3-4

[20] Karzes, T. Tiling fractal curves published online at:

http://www.karzes.com/xfract/xfract.html

[21] Kayne, Brian. H. *A Random Walk Through Fractal Dimensions*. John Wiley & Sons, Jul 11, 2008 - Technology & Engineering

[22] Mandelbrot, B. *The Fractal Geometry of Nature*. W. H. Freeman and Company. 1977

[23] McKenna, Douglas, M. SquaRecurves, E-Tours, Eddies and Frenzies: Basic Families of Peano Curves on the Square Grid, In: Guy, Richard K., Woodrow, Robert E.: The Lighter Side of Mathematics: Proceedings of the Eugene Strens Memorial Conference on Recreational Mathematics and its History, pp. 49-73, Mathematical Association of America, 1994

[24] Moore, E.H., On Certain Crinkly Curves, Trans Amer. Math Soc., 1, 72-90 (1900)

[25] Peano, G. "Sur une courbe, qui remplit toute une aire plane", *Mathematische Annalen* 36 (1): 157–160. 1890

[26] Prusinkiewicz, P. and Lindenmayer, A. *The Algorithmic Beauty of Plants*. Springer, 1990

[27] Radin. C (May 1994). "The Pinwheel Tiling of the Plane". *Annals of Mathematics*. 139 (3): 661-702. 2007-10-25.

[28] Ryde, K. Draft papers: "Iterations of the Dragon Curve" (https:// download.tuxfamily.org/user42/dragon/dragon.pdf), 2017; "Iterations of the R5 Dragon Curve" (https://download.tuxfamily.org/user42/ r5dragon/r5dragon.pdf) 2018; "Iterations of the Terdragon Curve" (https://download.tuxfamily.org/user42/terdragon/ terdragon.pdf), 2018.

[29] Sagan, Hans. *Space-filling Curves*. Springer Science and Business Media, 2012.

[30] Schraa, W. Range Fractal, published online at: http:// wolter.home.xs4all.nl/index.html

[31] Stange, K. Visualizing the Arithmetic of Imaginary Quadratic Fields. *International Mathematics Research Notices*, Volume 2018, Issue 12, 13 June 2018, Pages 3908–3938

[32] Steeman, Dieter. K. personal communication (http:// demonstrations.wolfram.com/author.html?author=Dieter+Steemann)

[33] Teachout, G. Spacefilling curve designs featured on the web site: http:// teachout1.net/village/

[34] Tricot, Claude. Curves and Fractal Dimension. Springer Science & Business Media, Nov.18, 1994. Mathematics.

[35] Ventrella, J. *Brainfilling Curves - A Fractal Bestiary*. Eyebrain Books/Lulu Press, 2012

[36] Ventrella, J. Portraits from the Family Tree of Plane-filling Curves. Proceedings of Bridges 2019: Mathematics, Art, Music, Architecture, Education, Culture. 2019.

[37] Weisstein, E. W. "Peano-Gosper Curve". MathWorld. October, 31, 2013

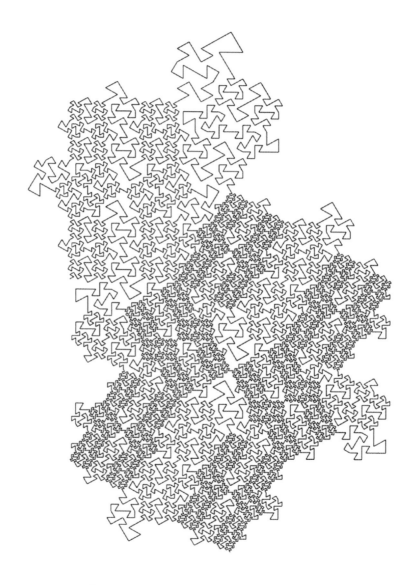

Figure 7. A self-avoiding curve of the $E(2,1)^2$ family

Printed in Great Britain
by Amazon

28787369R00088